THE FAMILY TREE OF THERESA JACQUELINE ANN PIDSLEY

Copyright - The Family Tree of Theresa Jacqueline Ann Pidsley ©
2022 Brian Parker. All rights reserved.

All rights reserved. No part of this book may be reproduced in any form or by an electronic or mechanical means including information storage and retrieval systems, without permission in writing from the author.
The only exception is by a reviewer, who may quote short excepts in a review.

Theresa Jacqueline Ann Pidsley Family Tree

Before I start there are a few things you need to know about the information given.

The public census started in **1841** and has been done every ten years, so far up to 2011 and list's all the people that were in the property on the night of the census. They could be the owner, family member, lodger or servant etc. (as long as they were in the address on the night of the census, even though they might normally live somewhere else). Due to the 100-year rule, we only have access to the 1841 – 1911 censuses for the moment; the 1921 being released soon.

Also, on the 29th September 1939, just before WW2 there was a register taken of all the people in the UK. This was done for the purpose of I.D. cards and food coupons etc. This register is better than a census as it gives dates of birth, not just the year like in a census.

The area's stated on a record (birth, marriage and death) is the place it was **registered** **(not always the location where the event took place).**

The spelling of the people's names, place names, dates and ages are as written on the records but are not always correct. Sometimes they couldn't write or even knew how old they were.

Another point is, the original records were handwritten and then at a later date transcribed on to computer records. During this process, mistakes were made in the spellings, making it hard sometimes to find a person.

Names in red are paternal side of the family
Names in blue are maternal side of the family

IT MUST BE STATED THAT BOTH GRAND MOTHERS, (PATERNAL) BEATRICE LYDIA ROSE POND and (MATERNAL) LILY FLORENCE POND ARE SISTERS AND THEREFORE HAVE THE SAME PARENTS. FROM THEIR PART OF THE TREE AND DOWN THIS SIDE OF THE FAMILY LINE THEY HAVE THE SAME GRANDPARENTS, ETC. SO, THESE RELATIONS NAMES I HAVE DONE IN PURPLE

PARENTS
EDWARD JOHN PIDSLEY & ANN ROSEMARY BRYARS

GRANDPARENTS
ERNEST RICHARD PIDSLEY & BEATRICE LYDIA ROSE POND
ERNEST HARRY BRYARS & LILY FLORENCE POND

GREAT GRANDPARENTS
RICHARD HENRY PIDSLEY & MARY JANE TUCKER
HERBERT D. POND & NORAH LYDIA FORD
WILLIAM HUDSON BRYARS & JESSIE FRANCES ELIZABETH CLARKE

2X GREAT GRANDPARENTS
RICHARD PIDSLEY & SUSAN VEYSEY / GARD
THOMAS TUCKER & MARY OTTON
EPHRAIM POND & MARY ANN ORAM
ELI FORD & JANE MASELEN
WILLIAM BRYARS & MARY ANN HUDSON
WILLIAM CLARKE & ELIZABETH DAKIN

3X GREAT GRANDPARENTS
HENRY PIDSLEY & HARRIET SKINNER
JOHN VERSEY & JULIA NEWBERRY
ROBERT TUCKER & MARY FRY
HENRY OTTON & JANE MOORE
THOMAS POND & ANN GARRETT
THOMAS ORAM & SARAH WILLIS
JOHN FORD & ELIZABETH ROLFE
JOHN BRYARS & ELIZABETH ELWICK
JONATHAN DAKIN & MARY SMITH

4X GREAT GRANDPARENTS
RICHARD PIDSLEY & SUSANNA FODDER
WILLIAM TUCKER & ELIZABETH SPURWAY
THOMAS POND & MARTHA GARRETT
RICHARD GARRETT & ANN WEBB
ISAAC ORAM & ANNE TAILOR
UNKNOWN & ELIZABETH WILLIS
JOHN FORD & MARY MOORE
SAMUEL ROLFE & ROSANNA FRANCES
WILLIAM ELWICK & SARAH SPENCER
THOMAS DAKIN & ELIZABETH MARSHALL

5X GREAT GRANDPARENTS
RICHARD TUCKER & MARY WILLIS
RICHARD SPURWAY & ELIZABETH (surname unknown)
JOHN POND & MARY BREACHER
CHRISTOPHER GARRETT & SARAH BRIDGES
JOHN MOORE & MARY BLANCHETT
WILLIAM ELWICK & MARY GARLAND
SAMUEL SPENCER & ELIZABETH KEYWORTH
THOMAS MARSHALL & JANE TAYLOR

6X GREAT GRANDPARENTS
JOHN MOOR/MOORE & DEBORAH AMOR
WILLIAM ELWICK & SARAH STANDRING
WILLIAM KEYWORTH & ANN MAILS

7X GREAT GRANDPARENTS
JOHN ELWICK & ELIZABETH GRAYS

THERESA JACQUELINE ANN PIDSLEY

Theresa was born on Monday the 11th April 1960 to parents Edward John and Ann Rosemary Pidsley (nee Bryars) .

Then in April 1980 in the registration district of Cirencester Theresa married Michael Austin.

They had two children, first a daughter Jodie Ann Austin born on Friday the 19th November 1982, in Cambridge.

On Saturday the 1st June 2013 at Milton Hill House, Milton Hill, Abingdon, Jodie married Robert Marc Gray (born on Tuesday the 8th February 1976 in Birmingham).

<u>Jodie Ann Austin and Robert Marc Gray</u>

They had two children: Chloe Ann born on Wednesday the 18th March 2015 in Chipping Norton and Joshua Roger born on Tuesday the 29th October 2019, in Banbury.

Jodie – Robert – Chloe – Joshua

Robert Marc Gray had two children by his first marriage, Jacob Marc born on Monday the 15th October 2001 and Thalia Jayne born on Monday the 13th September 2004, both in Banbury.

From left to right:
Jack Cowley, Craig Cowley, Gary Cowley, David Austin, Terry Steel, Paula Cowley, Louise Cowley and Jodie Gray

Theresa's and Michael's second child was a son, David Edward Austin born on Friday the 16th March 1984 in Cambridge.

David married Rose Mary Segal

Rose Mary Austin (nee Segal)

They have two children: Theo Daniel born on Saturday the 16th March 2019 and Rafael David born on Wednesday the 19th May 2021.

Theresa and Michael were divorced in 1993.

Then on Saturday the 15th October 1994, Theresa had a Church blessing in Shipton under Wychwood, marrying Christopher Michael Cowley, by the Rev. Canning.

<u>Christopher Michael Cowley</u>

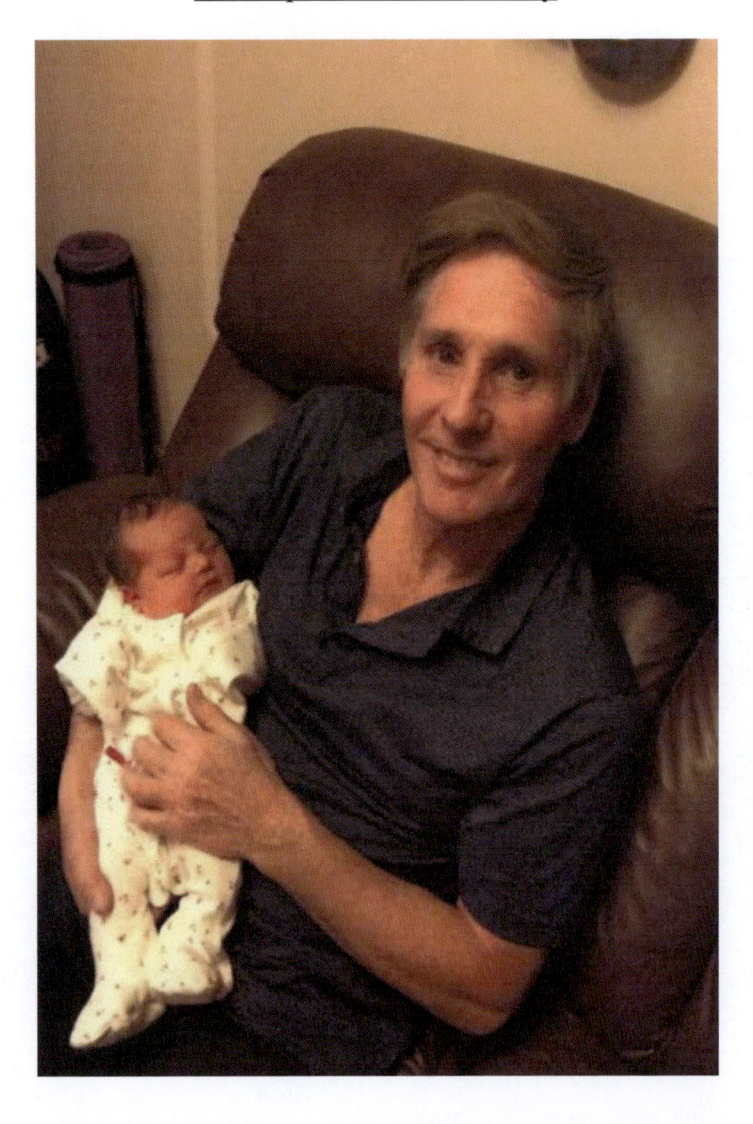

Christopher and Theresa Cowley

Theresa and Christopher then had a son, Craig Christopher born on Monday the 31st January 1994.

Craig's partner is Danielle Joyce Sadler who was born on Thursday the 2nd June 1988 and registered in the district of Oxford, with the mother's maiden name of Membury.

They have a daughter Holly Joyce Cowley born on Tuesday the 8th March 2022.

Craig Christopher Cowley

Craig, Danielle and Holly

Then Theresa and Christopher had a daughter, Louise Jacqueline on Thursday the 27th November 1997.

Louise Jacqueline Cowley

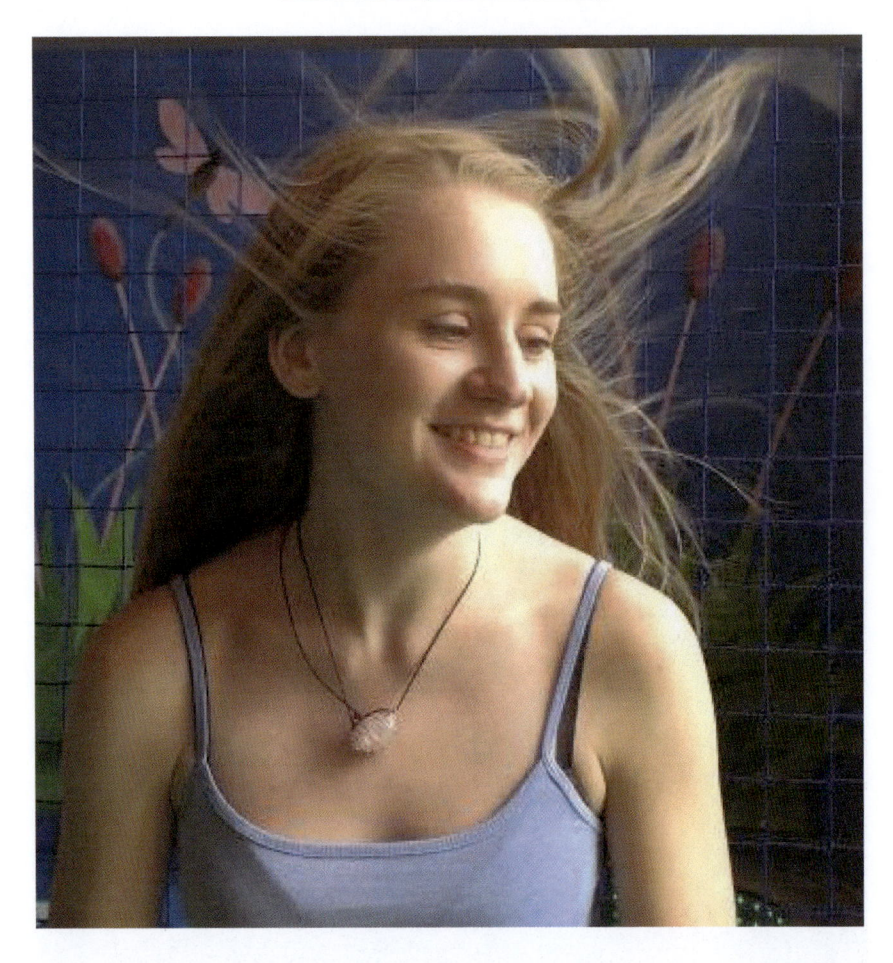

Louise Jacqueline Cowley

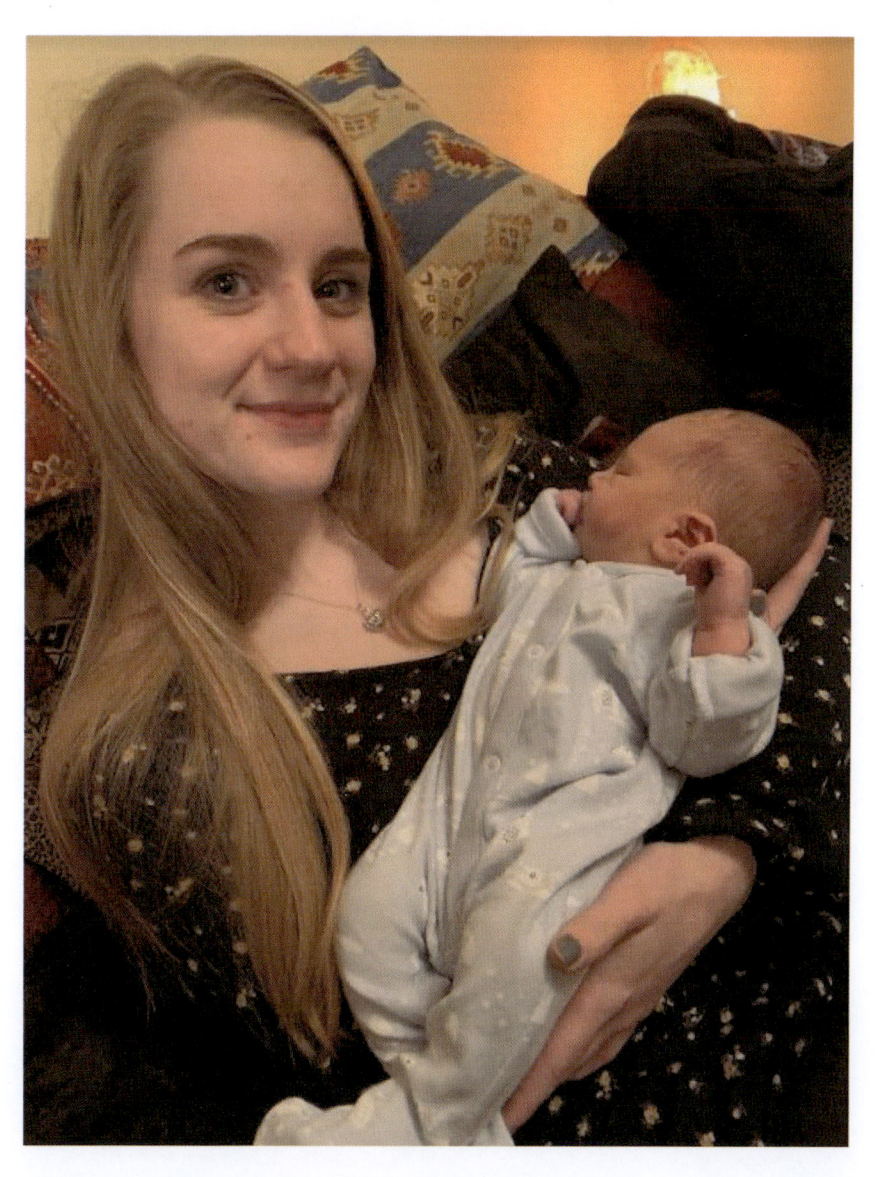

Theresa with her mother Ann Pidsley (nee Bryars)

Theresa and Christopher

Notes on Christopher Michael Cowley

Christopher was born on Thursday the 7th June 1956 in the registration district of Ashbourne, Derbyshire. In 1980 he married Susan Thake. They then had three children: Paula 1982, Gary 1983 and Jack 1988, all registered in the district of Cambridge. Gary has a daughter Savannah and Paula a son Jamie Charles.

Left to Right: Gary - Paula - Jack

Christopher's parents were Roy and Joan Dorothy Cowley (nee Jones). Roy Cowley was born on Wednesday the 12th August 1936 at 8 Market Street, Paddock, Huddersfield, and died on Saturday the 22 September 2018 in Norfolk. Joan was born on Wednesday the 18th September 1929.

Roy Cowley

Joan Dorothy Cowley (nee Jones)

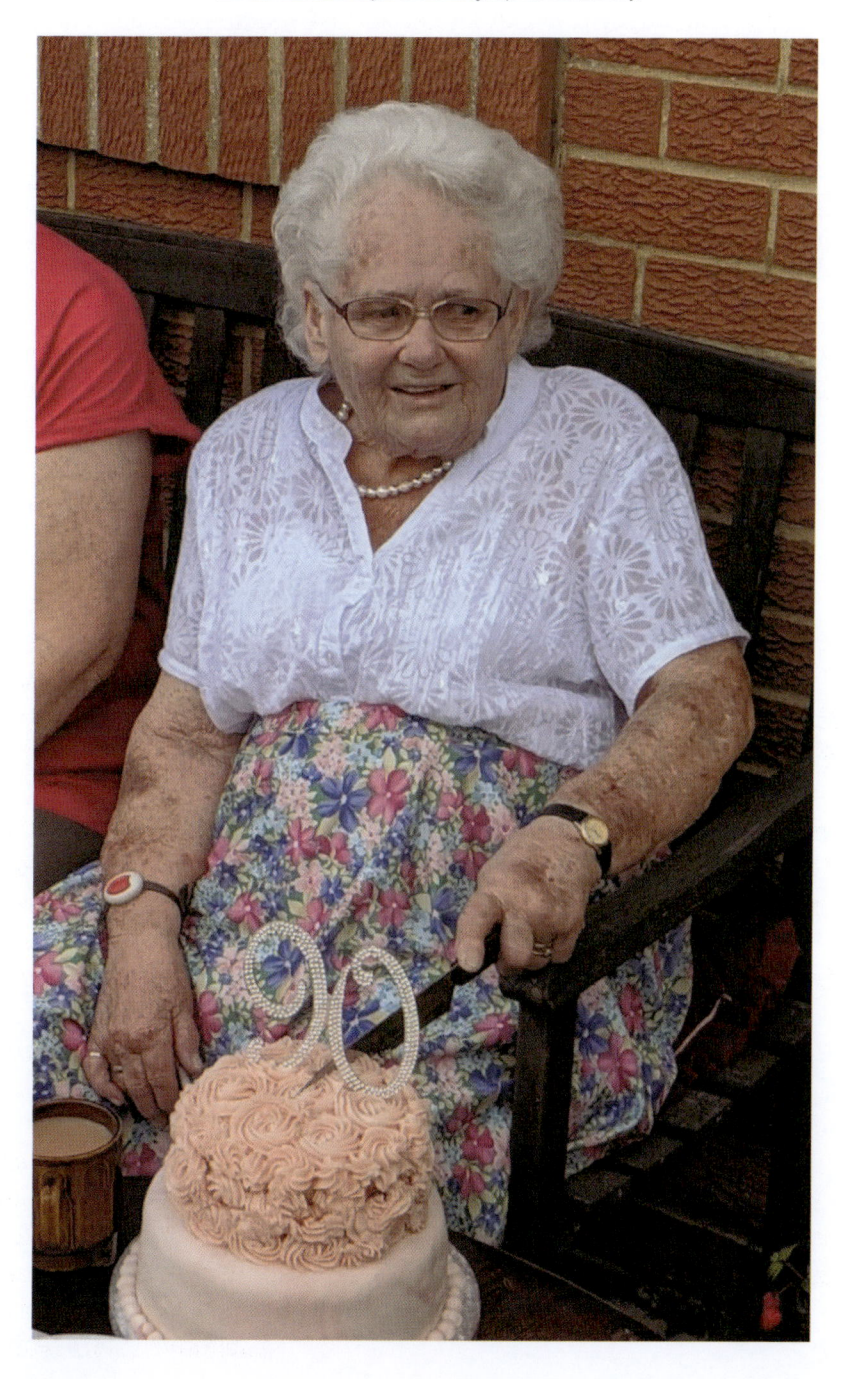

Theresa's family, left to right back row first:

Jodie Gray, Theresa Cowley, Mandy Christine Hale, Alison Lewis, Emma McLennan, Christine McLennan, Emily Hale, Helen Segal, Rosie Hale, Louise Cowley, Rose Austin Segal and Thalia Gray.

PARENTS
EDWARD JOHN PIDSLEY & ANN ROSEMARY BRYARS

EDWARD JOHN PIDSLEY
Edward was born on Thursday the 21st April 1932 in Edmonton, Essex, to parents Ernest Richard and Beatrice Lydia Rose Pidsley (nee Pond).

On the 1939 register he is aged 7, living with his parents and sibling Richard Henry. There was also somebody else in the house, but the name is blanked out. The address was in the district of Beverstone, near Tetbury.

He was married in Q2 of 1954 in the district of Caerleon, Monmouthshire, to Ann Rosemary Bryars.

Edward and Ann

Edward and Ann

On the Electoral Register of 1955, he is shown as living with his wife at 202 Wellington Road, Edmonton. Also in the house was Gladys Warren.

202 Wellington Road

They had three children: Brian J. born on Saturday the 5th April 1958.

Brian Pidsley

Then Theresa Jaqueline Ann, on Monday the 11th April 1960 and Steven Edward, on Friday the 5th February 1965.

Edward John Pidsley died in 1992 aged 60 in the registration district of Oxford.

Notes on Edward and Ann's children

Brian J. married Angela Maria Talty on the 20th April 1985 in the registration district of West Oxfordshire.

Angela Maria Talty and Brian Pidsley

Angela Maria Pidsley (nee Talty)

They had two children, Gemma Louise born on the 22nd February 1988.

<u>Gemma Louise Pidsley</u>

Then Martin John, born on the 17th January 1990.

Gemma married Oliver Richard Huke on the 21ˢᵗ August 2021.

Oliver Richard Huke

They have a son, Logan Peter Huke born on the 22nd April 2021.

<u>Logan Peter Huke</u>

<u>Steven Edward</u> married Julie E. Tuppenney in Ploughley, Oxfordshire. They had four children: Adam Peter 1988, Robert E. 1990, Mark A. 1991 and Alex Joshua 1996.

ANN ROSEMARY BRYARS

Ann was born on Monday the 9th October 1932 in Newport, Glamorganshire, to parents Ernest Harry and Lily Florence Bryars (nee Pond).

She had an older sidling Norah Elizabeth Joy (1921-1997) and then later another sibling John Hudson (1934-1997).

She was married in Q2 of 1954 in the district of Caerleon, Monmouthshire, to Edward John Pidsley.

On the Electoral Register for 2003-2009 she was living at 29 Sinnels Field, Shipton-Under-Wychwood.

Ann died on Sunday the 1st June 2014 in the registration district of Chipping Norton, and was buried at Saint Mary the Virgin, Shipton-Under-Wychwood.

GRANDPARENTS
ERNEST RICHARD PIDSLEY & BEATRICE LYDIA ROSE POND

ERNEST RICHARD PIDSLEY
Ernest was born on Saturday the 7th July 1888 in Ashprington, Devon, to parents Richard Henry and Mary Jane Pidsley (nee Tucker).
On the 1891 census he is aged 2, with his parents and two siblings: Ethel Victoria Mary aged 3 and Christina of 6 months. Also in the property was Emma Hern (cousin) and William Brown (Servant-Journeyman-Baker). They were living in the Ashprington Post Office. In the next census of 1901, he is aged 12 and listed as one of the twenty-one scholars' at the Cathedral School in Cathedral Yard, Exeter.

He is aged 22 now on the 1911 census and listed as a boarder in the 86 Dudley Road, Grantham, Lincolnshire. His occupation was "Watch Makers Assistant."

In WW1 he was in the North Somerset Yeomanry, 13th Rifle Brigade with the Regimental Number of 666. He received the 1914 Star & clasp.

Ernest Richard Pidsley

Later on, he is in the WW1 Rolls of Honour, and is listed as "Temp / Lieutenant".

Roll of Honour

> T./Lt. Ernest Richard Pidsley, Rif. Brig.
> For conspicuous gallantry and initiative during operations. He carried out many daring reconnaissances under heavy fire. The information which he obtained was always of great value and on more than one occasion was essential to the success of the operations.

On Tuesday the 6th February 1917 in Gabalfa, Glamorganshire, he married Winifred Janie Gill. On the marriage certificate it shows him as aged 29, a Bachelor with his occupation as "Second Lieutenant" in the 13th Rifle Brigade. His address at the time was 10 Haldon Road, Exeter, and his father was Richard Henry Pidsley with occupation of "Superintendent". Winifred was aged 30, a Spinster, living at 98 Newfoundland Road, Gabalfa. Her father was George Chubb Gill who was a "Carpenter." The witnesses to the marriage were Richard Henry and Mary Jane Pidsley who were his Father & Mother.

Marriage certificate

1917. Marriage solemnized at St Mark's Church in the Parish of Gabalfa in the County of Glamorgan

No.	When Married	Name and Surname	Age	Condition	Rank or Profession	Residence at the time of Marriage	Father's Name and Surname	Rank or Profession of Father
238	February Sixth 1917	Ernest Richard Priestley	29	Bachelor	Sec. Lieutenant in its 5th Batt Rifle Brigade	10 Mallow Road Exeter	Richard Henry Priestley	Superintendent
		Winifred Louise Gill	30	Spinster	—	98 Westmoreland Lane Gabalfa	Albert H Gill	Carpenter

Married in the Church of St Mark according to the Rites and Ceremonies of the Established Church, by Licence by me, L.W. Egerton Priestley

This Marriage was solemnized between us, { Ernest Richard Priestley / Winifred Louise Gill } in the Presence of us, { R H Priestley Mary Louise Priestley / George Church Lizzie Eleanor Alewin Hill }

I cannot find any birth of a child with the name Pidsley and the mother's maiden name of Gill, so suspect they had no children

At some time, they must have separated as in Q2 of 1929 in the district of Melksham, Wiltshire, Ernest Richard Pidsley had a son named Ernest George Pidsley and the mother's maiden name was given as "Pond". This was followed on Friday the 7th November 1930 by another son Richard Henry Pidsley born in the district of Hendon and again the mother's maiden name was given as "Pond". Then a third son **Edward John Pidsley born on Thursday the 21st April 1932 (your father)**. The mothers name was again "Pond."

Ernest was then married in Q3 1934 in the district of Edmonton, Essex to Beatrice Lydia Rose Pond.

They then had two more children: William in 1934 and Christine Rose in 1946.

On the 1939 register he is listed as being with his wife and three other people who were:- Richard Henry and Edward John with the third name blanked out (suspect it is Ernest George). They were living in Beverston, Tetbury. His occupation was given as "Director & Sales Manager."

Ernest died on Wednesday the 18th July 1951 in Worksop Kilton Hospital, Worksop, Nottingham.

His probate (shown below) gives his address as 63 The Orchard, London N.21

<u>Probate</u>

PIDSLEY Ernest Richard of 63 The Orchard **London N.21** died 18 July 1951 at Worksop Kilton Hospital Worksop Nottinghamshire Administration (with Will) **London** 13 October to Beatrice Rose Pidsley widow. Effects £3950.

NOTES ON HIS FIRST WIFE

Winifred Janie Gill was born in 1885 in the district of Cardiff.
In the 1939 register she was listed as "Divorced and living at 59 Cae Gwyn Road, Cardiff, with the occupation of "Assistant Superintendent in Dyers & Cleaners". On the 1949 Electoral Register she was living at 16 Ton-Yr-Ywen Avenue, Cardiff. She died on Monday the 2nd October 1972, living at Longford Cottage, Stroud, Gloucester. She was still using the name Gill-Pidsley.

NOTES ON HIS CHILDREN

Ernest George was born in Q2 1929 in the district of Melksham, Wiltshire.
On the London electoral register for the years between 1950- 1963, he was living at 63 The Orchard, Edmonton. In the house between these dates, he is with his mother Beatrice and sometimes his brothers Richard and William.

Richard Henry was born on 7th November 1930 and registered in the district of Hendon, Greater London. He was married in Q3 1956 in the district of the Isle of Wight, to Marcia Christine Porcelli. They had two children, Kevin Richard born 1956 in the district of Croydon and Amanda Marcia born 1963 in the Edmonton, Essex, district. Richard was remarried in 1975 to Eileen Versey in the district of Westminster, London. The electoral register for 2003-2004 shows they were living at 133 Manners Way, Southend-on Sea.
He died in 2005 in Southend-on Sea.

Richard Henry Pidsley

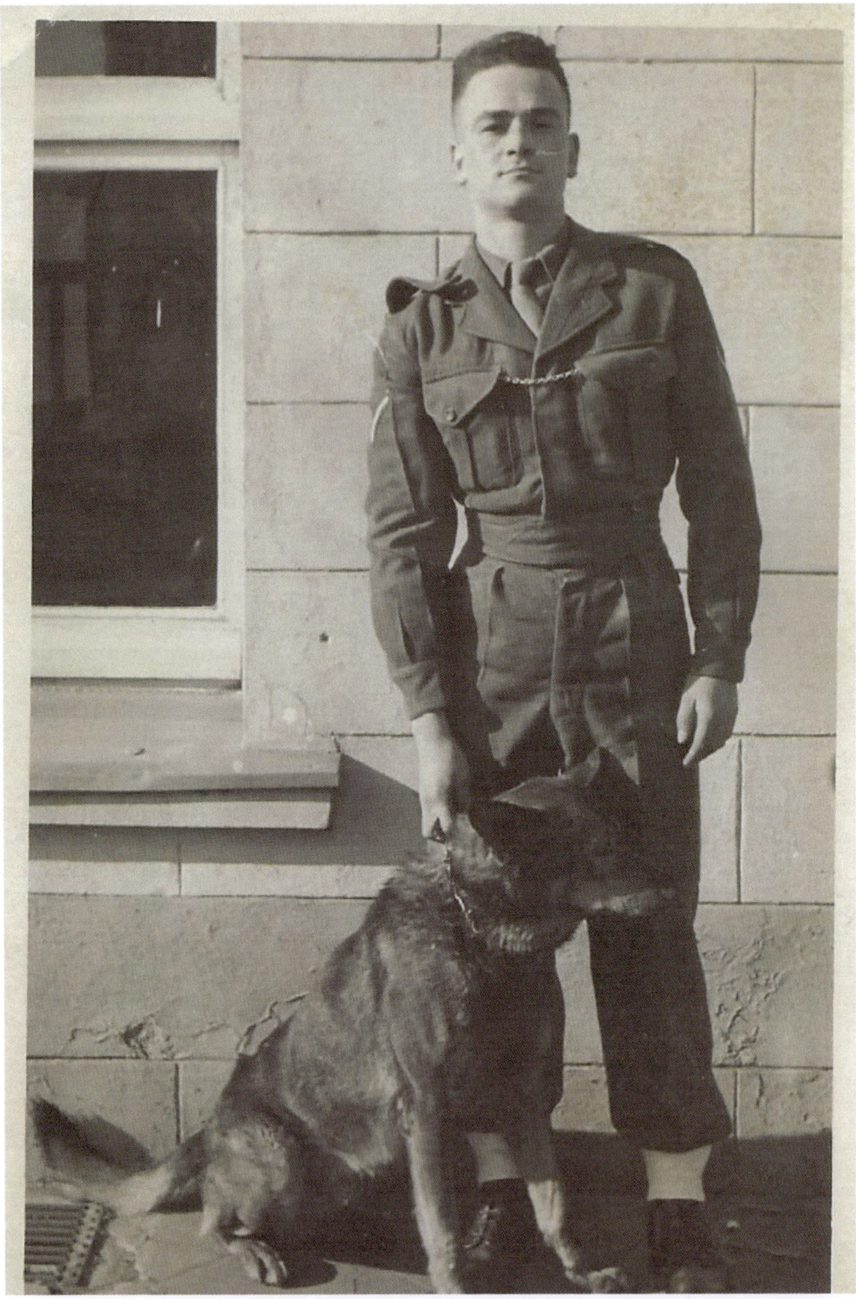

William Rupert was born in 1934 and registered in Edmonton, Essex. He married in 1961 in Epping, Essex to Margaret Taylor. They had three children Mark William 1962, Alison Elizabeth born on the 8th June 1965 in Epping, Enfield, and Judith Margaret in 1967.
Alison Elizabeth was married in June 1991 at St. Josephs, Huddersfield, to Philip Antony Lewis (born 12th February 1965 in Slough). They had two children: Kathryn Ann Lewis born on the 18th July 1993 in Huddersfield Royal Infirmary and Timothy Mark born on the 9th August 1996 in the Worcester Royal.

Christine Rose was born 1945 in the district of Edmonton. She married Alexander S. McLennan in Q2 1967 in Enfield., They had a son, James Scott McLennan in 1970 in the district of Maldon, Essex who in the district of Colchester married Emma L. Wrenn in 2003. Then a daughter, Caroline Olivia McLennan in 1976 in the district of Brentwood, Essex, who in the district of Chelmsford married Mark T. Brooks in 2004.

BEATRICE LYDIA ROSE POND

Beatrice was born on Friday the 23rd September 1904 in Paddington, London, to parents Herbert David and Norah Lydia Pond (nee Ford).

On the 1911 census she is aged 6, with her parents and three siblings: Lily Florence 14, Ethel May 11 and Ivy Gladys Gwendoline 1. They lived at 20 Church Place, Paddington Green.

She was married in Q3 1934 in the district of Edmonton, Essex to Ernest Richard Pidsley.

Her husband Ernest Richard died in 1951.

On the Electoral register for 1954 she was living at 63 The Orchard Road, Edmonton.

Beatrice died on Friday the 5th December 1980 in the district of Dewsbury, but her probate shows her address as being 133 Manners Way, Southend-on-Sea.

Probate

PIDSLEY, Beatrice Lydia Rose of 133 Manners Wy Sout: nd-on-Sea died 5 December 1980 Probate Ipswich 2 April £16889 811003556K

133 Manners Way

GRANDPARENTS
ERNEST HARRY BRYARS & LILY FLORENCE POND

ERNEST HARRY BRYARS
Ernest was born on Monday the 25th December 1893 in Sheffield, to parents William Hudson and Jessie Francis Bryars (nee Clarke).

Ernest's Baptism and Confirmation

Be thou faithful unto Death and I will give thee a crown of Life

Baptized: Ernest Harry Bryars — 21 Jan. 1894 — Attercliffe Church.

Confirmed: 28 February 1910 — Darnall Church

First Communion: 6 March 1910 — Attercliffe Parish Church

Signed: J. Lee Nicholls

A Daily Prayer

Almighty and Everliving GOD, defend me, Thy servant, with Thy heavenly Grace, that I may continue Thine for ever; and daily increase in Thy Holy Spirit more and more, until I come unto Thine Everlasting Kingdom, through our Lord Jesus Christ. Amen.

S.P.C.K.

He was aged 7 on the 1901 census, living with his parents and four siblings: William Hudson 10, Arthur 8, Mary Elizabeth 5, Francis 3 and John Fair Fax 10 months. The house was on the Athercliffe Road, Athercliffe cum Darnall, Sheffield.

Ernest in the Boys Brigade

In the next census in 1911 he is aged 17 and listed as "Nephew" to the householder who was Edith Annie Earnshaw. The address was 31 Godolphin Road, Shepherds Bush, London. He is listed as "Commercial Student."

31 Godolphin Road

In WW1 he enlisted in the Army on Friday the 4th September 1914, first of all in the 3rd London Regiment as a Private with service number 2608 and then in the Labour Corp with service number 342692. He received the Victory Medal, British War Medal and the 1914- 15 Star. On the WW1 Pension Records, he is shown as a Lance Corporal in the Labour Corp and was discharged with Disability on Tuesday the 29th April 1919 in Newport, Monmouthshire, Wales. As he was being discharged with a disability he would have also received "The Silver War Badge." On the back of this medal would be stamped a personal number. His was B282827

ORIGINAL

29 ROLL OF INDIVIDUALS entitled to the "WAR BADGE"

No. .... WAR OFFICE

65411

Regtl. No.	Rank	Name (in full)	Unit discharged from	No. of Badge and Certificates (To be completed at War Office)	Date of :— Enlistment	Date of :— Discharge	Cause of Discharge (Wounds or Sickness and para. of K.R.)	Whether served Overseas (Yes or No)
282926	Pte	Dingwall, Alexander	Labour Corps	B/272823	15.11.11	19.3.19	Sick Para 392	Yes
345682	"	Barr, Wm. Arthur	Labour Corps	B.282,824	7.9.14	15.7.19	"	"
341299	"	Irving, John	Labour Corps	B.282,825	16.6.14	21.6.19	"	"
342176	"	Sanders, Harry	Labour Corps	B.282,826	23.11.14	5.4.19	"	"
342692	L/C	Bryans, Ernest H.	Labour Corps	B.282,827	7.7.14	29.4.19	"	"
345447	A/Cpl	Bailey, Geo. F.	Labour Corps	B.282,828	29.11.10	12.6.19	"	"
345690	Sgt	Chappell, Fredk. G.	Labour Corps	B.282,829	31.8.14	18.2.19	"	"
346459	"	Ellis, James	Labour Corps	B.282,830	23.11.14	27.6.19	"	"
346491	A/Sgt	Bunfleet, Wm. A.	Labour Corps	B.282,831	11.6.14	15.7.19	"	"
346840	ACQMS	Press, Herbert Geo	Labour Corps	B.282,832	12.6.12	4.7.19	"	"
256175	Pte	Harris, Arthur E.	Labour Corps	B.282,833	30.11.14	15.3.19	"	"
200779	"	Kingham, Albert John	Labour Corps	M/P.2544	17.9.14	11.3.19	"	"

I certify that the particulars furnished hereon are correct.

Date: ....

Place: Nottingham

I certify that Badges and Certificates numbered as above, have been issued to the individuals concerned.

Date: ....

Signature and Rank of Officer certifying Claimants' service.

Signature and Rank of Officer certifying issue.

Silver War Badge

The Silver War Badge was issued in the United Kingdom and the British Empire to service personnel who had been honourably discharged due to wounds or sickness from military service in World War I. The badge, sometimes known as the "Discharge Badge", the "Wound Badge" or "Services Rendered Badge", was first issued in September 1916, along with an official certificate of entitlement.

The large sterling silver lapel badge was intended to be worn on civilian clothes. The decoration was introduced as an award of "King's silver" for having received wounds or injury during loyal war service to the Crown's authority. A secondary causation for its introduction was that a practice had developed in the early years of the war in the United Kingdom where some women took it upon themselves to confront and publicly embarrass men of fighting age they saw in public places who were not in military uniform, by ostentatiously presenting them with white feathers, as a suggestion of cowardice. As the war had developed substantial numbers of servicemen who had been discharged from His Majesty's Forces with wounds that rendered them unfit for war service, but which were not obvious from their outward appearance, found themselves being harassed in such a manner and the badge, to be worn on the right breast while in civilian dress, was a means of discouraging such incidents being directed at ex-forces' personnel. It was forbidden to wear the badge on a military uniform.

Ernest Harry Bryars

On Wednesday, the 4th September 1918 he married Lily Florence Pond at St. Mary, Paddington Green, Westminster. He was aged 24 and a "Soldier" while she was aged 21. The witnesses were: Herbert Pond, Ethel Pond and Norah Pond.

Marriage certificate

1918. Marriage solemnized at S. Mary's Church of S. Mary's Littlehampton in the Parish in the County of Sussex

No.	When Married	Name and Surname	Age	Condition	Rank or Profession	Residence at the time of Marriage	Father's Name and Surname	Rank or Profession of Father
242	September 4th 1918	Ernest Westby Bryant	44	Bachelor	Soldier	S. Peter's, Brandy Mount	William Hudson Bryant (deceased)	Clergyman
		Ada Florence Pond	21	Spinster	—	21 Church Place	Herbert Smith Pond	Surveyor

Married in the Parish Church according to the Rites and Ceremonies of the Established Church, by after Banns by me,

This Marriage was solemnized between us, { Ernest Westby Bryant / Ada Florence Pond } in the Presence of us, { Herbert T. Pond, Robt Pond, Ada Lydia Pond, H. R. Mullins } Reginald Trevor, Curate.

On the 1939 register he is aged 46, living with his wife and two other people, one being their son John Hudson and the other one blanked out but possibly their daughter Ann Rosemary. Ernest's occupation was given as "Drapers Window Dresser." Additionally, as it was the time of WW2, he was also an Air Raid Warden. They lived at 14 Brynderwen Road, Newport, Monmouthshire.

Ernest died in Q1 1977 in the registration district of Brecknock, Powys, Wales.

Notes on their three children:

Nora Elizabeth Joy
Nora was born on Saturday the 12th March 1921 in the registration district of Paddington. On Saturday the 20th July in 1946 she was married to Leslie Gilbert Whitworth in Newport, Monmouthshire. Nora died on Monday the 28th July 1997 in the registration district of Kidderminster. Her husband Leslie was born on Monday the 9th June 1919 in Westbury, Shropshire and died on Saturday the 21st July 1990 in Bristol. He was living at 66 South Liberty Lane, Ashton Vale, Bristol.
They had two children:
The first was Heather Susan Whitworth born on Monday the 9th February 1948 and then who was married on Sunday the 23rd September 1967 at St. Aldhelm's Church, Bedminster, Bristol, to Alan John Bird. They had three children: Nicola Tracey 1968, Andrea Louise 1971 and James Alexander 1976. Heather died on Saturday the 1st October 2011.
The second was Michael Robin Whitworth born on Saturday the 29th December 1951. He married Jacqueline Herod on Saturday the 8th February 1975 in Bristol Registry Office.

Ann Rosemary (your mother) 1932-2014

John Hudson.
John was born on Saturday the 24th February 1934 in Newport. He is listed on the Out-Going Passengers List. On Wednesday the 20th May 1959 he was departing Glasgow Port bound for Wellington, New Zealand. It gives his date of birth as 24th February 1934, his address as 4 Park Close, Alton, Hampshire and his occupation was "Electrician". The ship was the T.S.S. Captain Cook, which was owned by the New Zealand Government to bring British migrants to New Zealand between 1952 and 1959.

On this trip there were 803 people over the age of twelve, 226 between the ages of one and twelve and 25 under the age of one, making a total of 1054 emigrating.

"T.S.S.Captain Cook" in Wellington Harbour.

59747	SINGH	Mr.Alexander	"	M 26.4.36	M	23 Coltness St.,Rosehill Glasgow,E.2.	PAKISTAN	DOC. OF IMM.	U.K.
		Mrs.Irene	"	F 3.4.39	"	"	"	"	U.K.
59748	BRIANS	Mr.John	"	M 26.6.34	S	4 Park Close Rd.,Alton East	BLACKISTAN	U.K.	U.K.
59749	BUTLER	Mr.Attobie	"	M 13.9.13	M	12 Heathery Rd.,Wishaw Lanarkshire	HOLDEN	DOC. OF IMM.	SCOTLAND
		Mrs.Georgina	"	F 28.6.13	"	"	"	"	"

He was married about 1960 to Shelia Noble.
BUT HOW DID HE MEET HER.
Sheila was born on the Thursday the 13th of August 1936 in Newcastle upon Tyne, Northumberland. In early 1958 she was living at 40 Fairfield Green, Whitley Bay, Northumberland and was a "Civil Servant". Then on Tuesday the 25th February 1958 she is departing Glasgow Port bound for Wellington, New Zealand. On the same ship but at different times then her future husband did.

So, did they meet in New Zealand.

John is listed on the New Zealand electoral register for 1972 as living in Kapiti, Wellington, New Zealand. They returned to the UK and John died in 1997 in Bristol aged 63. Shelia died in Bristol on Wednesday the 29th of November 2009 aged 73.

They had a son Raymond born on Saturday the 14th October 1967 in New Zealand, but Raymond when aged 17 died on Saturday the 21st September 1985 in Bristol, of Leukaemia.

Raymond Hudson

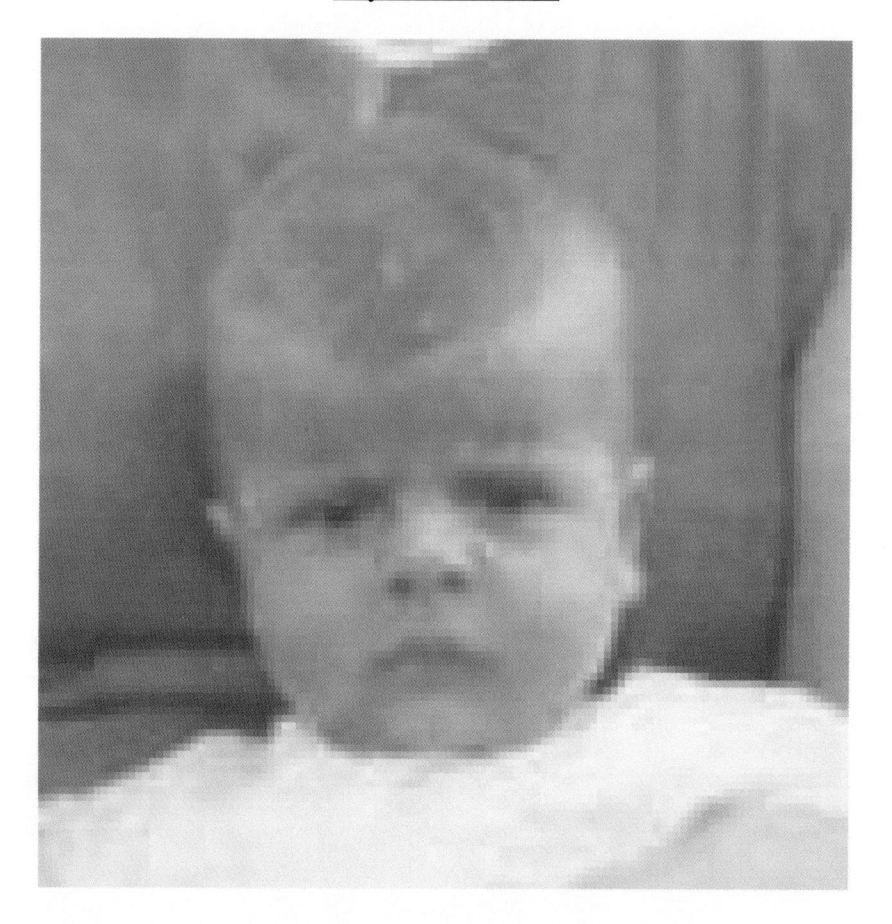

There was also another son but unable to find the name.

Ernest with his daughter Norah and wife Lily

It is **suspected** that the people in the photo are, at the Back - Frances, Front right – Mary, Front left - Lily Florence Bryars (nee Pond) and the baby is Norah Elizabeth, Ernest's and Lily's oldest child. As Norah was born in 1921, this must date the picture to this period and lily would be about twenty-four years old.

LILY FLORENCE POND

Lily was born on Monday the 21st September 1896 in Trowbridge, Wiltshire, to parents Herbert David and Norah Lydia Pond (nee Ford). She is aged 4 on the 1901 census, living with her parents and sister Ethel M. aged 1. The address was 19 Church Place in Paddington, London.

The Schools Admissions and Discharge Register shows Lily Florence Pond (she was aged 9) as being admitted to Marylebone Saint James School on Monday the 16th October 1905 with her house address as 19 Church Place. Her father was Herbert Pond, her date of birth as 21st September 1896. It also revealed that the last school she attended was Saint Michaels. It also states that she had been in Saint James for a few months, writes fairly well but reads badly, arithmetic poor.

Now aged 14 in the 1911 census she is with her parents and three younger siblings: Ethel May 11, Beatrice Lydia 6 and Ivy Gladys Gwendoline 1. They lived at 20 Church Place, Paddington Green.

On Wednesday the 4th September 1918, Lily Florence married Ernest Harry Bryars at St. Mary, Paddington Green, Westminster.
Lily died in Q1 1951 in Newport, Gwent.

Lily Florence Bryars (nee Pond) on the right with her mother Norah Lydia Pond on the left and Herbert Maurice Pond, Lilys young brother.

~~~

GREAT GRANDPARENTS
RICHARD HENRY PIDSLEY & MARY JANE TUCKER

RICHARD HENRY PIDSLEY

Richard was born on Wednesday the 5th December 1860 and baptised on the 21st, in the district of Ottery Saint Mary, Devon, to parents Richard and Susan Pidsley (nee Gard – BUT SHE WAS BORN SUSAN VEYSEY AND THEN MARRIED Mr. Gard).

The 1871 census shows him aged 10. He is listed as "Nephew and **Orphan**" to the householder who was his uncle and a farmer of two hundred acres, employing five men, two sons and two boys. This was in Sowton, Devon.

He is aged 20 on the next census in 1881 and is listed as "Cousin" to the householder who was Arthur Pidsley, a farmer of two hundred and three acres employing three men and two boys. This was in Sowton, Devon. Richard is an "Assistant in Farming." This was in Sowton, Devon.

On Monday, the 27th September 1886 in Sowton parish Church he married Mary Jane Tucker.

Aged 30 in 1891 he is living with his wife and three children: Ethel Victoria Mary 3, **Ernest Richard. 2 (your Grandfather)** and Christina Harriet aged 6 months, living in Ashprington, Devon. His occupation was "Baker and Sub Postmaster."

He is now aged 40 on the 1901 census with his wife and two children: Ethel 13 and Dorothy Frances 3, living at 66 Saint Davids Hill, Exeter. His occupation was "Baker and Confectioner."

Then in 1911 he is now aged 50, living with his wife and daughter Dorothy. The address was 10 Haldon Road, Exeter, where he was an "Insurance Agent".

Richard Henry died in 1928 in Exeter.

NOTES ON THEIR CHILDREN

Ethel Victoria Mary was born 3rd July and baptised 4th August 1887 in Ashprington, Devon. Religion – Anglican.

Detail	
Name:	Ethel Victoria Mary Pidsley
Birth Date:	3 Jul 1887
Baptism Date:	4 Aug 1887
Baptism Place:	Ashprington, Devon, England
Religion:	Anglican
Search Photos:	Search for 'Ashprington' in the UK City, Town and Village Photos collection
Father:	Richard Henry Pidsley
Mother:	Mary Jane Pidsley

Then on the 23rd July 1911 in Exeter she married John Arthur Trotter (1882-1930).

Ethel Victoria Mary Pidsley
in the Devon, England, Church of England Marriages and Banns

Detail Source	
Name:	Ethel Victoria Mary Pidsley
Record Type:	Marriage Banns (Marriage Bann)
Marriage Banns Date:	23 Jul 1911
Marriage Banns Place:	Exeter, St David, Devon, England
Residence Date:	Abt 1911
Residence Place:	Exeter St David
Religion:	Anglican

Sometime after they emigrated to Canada. On the 24th January 1916 in Calgary, Canada she died aged 29. She is buried in the Union cemetery, Calgary, in Section "T," Block 1, Plot 47.

Ethel Mary Trotter

BIRTH	1888
DEATH	24 Jan 1916 (aged 27–28)
BURIAL	Union Cemetery
	Calgary, Calgary Census Division, Alberta, Canada
PLOT	Section T, Block 1, Plot 47
MEMORIAL ID	123753033 · View Source

MARY JANE TUCKER

Mary was born in 1859 in Honiton, Devon, to parents Thomas and Mary Tucker (nee Otton).

In the 1861 census she is aged 2, living with her parents in Honiton.

Then on the next census in 1871 she is listed as aged 12 and "Granddaughter" to the householder, who was Jane Otten aged 81, a "Retired Dairy Worker", living in Honiton.

Mary is now aged 22 in 1881, listed as "Niece" to the householders who was William Dawe and his wife Ann, living at 13 Bedford Circus, Exeter.

Pictures below show Bedford Circus. It was badly bombed on the 4th May 1942 and caught fire and in later years demolished.

Bedford Circus, Bristol

On Monday, the 27th September 1886 in Sowton parish Church she married Richard Henry Pidsley.
Her husband died in 1928.
Mary died in 1941 in Exeter.

GREAT GRANDPARENTS
HERBERT DAVID POND & NORAH LYDIA FORD

HERBERT DAVID POND
Herbert was born on Sunday the 30th May 1875 in Trowbridge , Wiltshire , to parents Ephraim and Mary Ann Pond (nee Oram).
On the 1881 census Herbert is aged 5, living with his parents at 50 Castle Street, Trowbridge.
Now aged 15 and living with his parents at 16 Polebarn Road, Trowbridge. His occupation was "Cloth Worker."

In Q2 1896 in Melksham, Wiltshire he married Norah Lydia Ford.

He is aged 26 on the 1901 census, living with his wife and two children: **Lily Florence 4 (your Maternal Grandmother)** and Ethel M. aged 1. The address was 19 Church Place in Paddington, London, and he was a "Brewers Storeman".

Looking at the Baptism records for London it shows that Lily Florence was born on the 21st September 1896, Ethel May was born on the 24th November 1899 and Beatrice Lydia Rose was born on the 23rd September 1904. But they were all baptised on the same day on the 16th October 1904 in the parish of St. Mary's, Paddington. Herbert is a "Storekeeper" and they lived at 19 Church Place, Paddington.

Then in 1911 he was aged 36, with his wife and four children: **Lily Florence 14 (your Maternal Grandmother)** and Ethel May. 11, **Beatrice Lydia Rose 6 (your Paternal Grandmother)** and Ivy Gwendoline aged 1. They lived now at 20 Church Place in Paddington, London, and he was an "Off License Manager".

In the 1939 register he is listed as living at 102 Frome Road, Trowbridge, with his wife and four other people of which two are blanked out. His occupation was "Brewers Storeman." Suspect this to be Ushers Brewery.

<u>Ushers Brewery lorry</u>

102 Frome Road

He died on Tuesday the 5th November 1946 and was buried in Saint John's Churchyard in Trowbridge.

Herbert David Pond's Grave

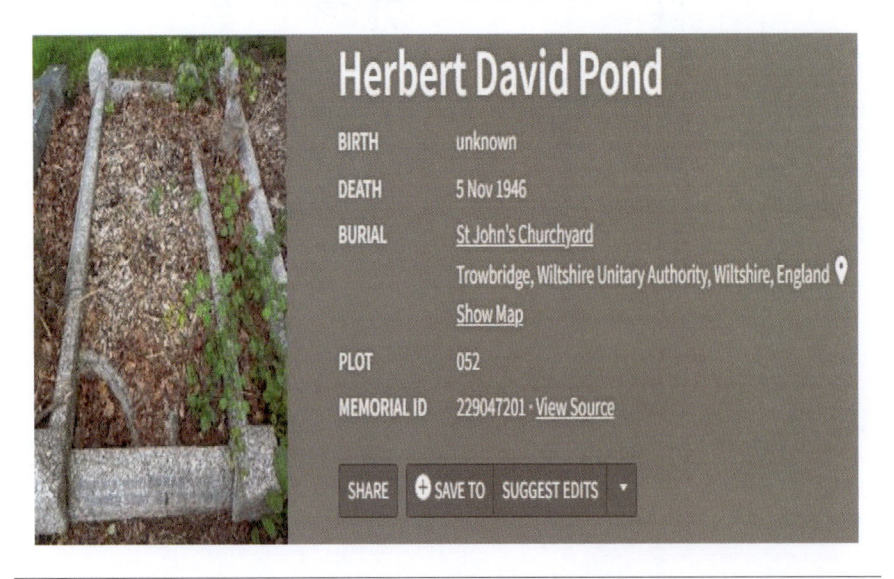

Herbert David Pond

BIRTH	unknown
DEATH	5 Nov 1946
BURIAL	St John's Churchyard
	Trowbridge, Wiltshire Unitary Authority, Wiltshire, England
	Show Map
PLOT	052
MEMORIAL ID	229047201 · View Source

SHARE SAVE TO SUGGEST EDITS

Probate

> **POND** Herbert David of 102 Frome-road Trowbridge **Wiltshire** died 6 November 1948 Administration **London** 30 December to Norah Lydia Pond widow. Effects £325 4s. 7d.

Notes

The 1911 census gives more information than the earlier census's. It tells how many children they had in their married lives and how many are still alive. In Herbert's and Norah's case it states: six children were born and four still living in 1911. The 1901 and 1911 census's shows four children and they are the ones still alive on the 1911 record. It must mean that the two dead children were born after 1896 but died before 1911. So, who were they? I can find in death records two children with the surname of "Pond" that were born in the registration district of London and were both born in 1906 and both died in Q3 of the same that year. Their names were Bertie and Elsie Dorothy. But cannot prove if they were Herbert's and Norah's children.

Also, Herbert and Norah did have another child - Herbert Maurice Douglas Pond. He was baptised on Sunday the 2nd September 1917 at St. Mary's, Paddington Green, London.

Birth record

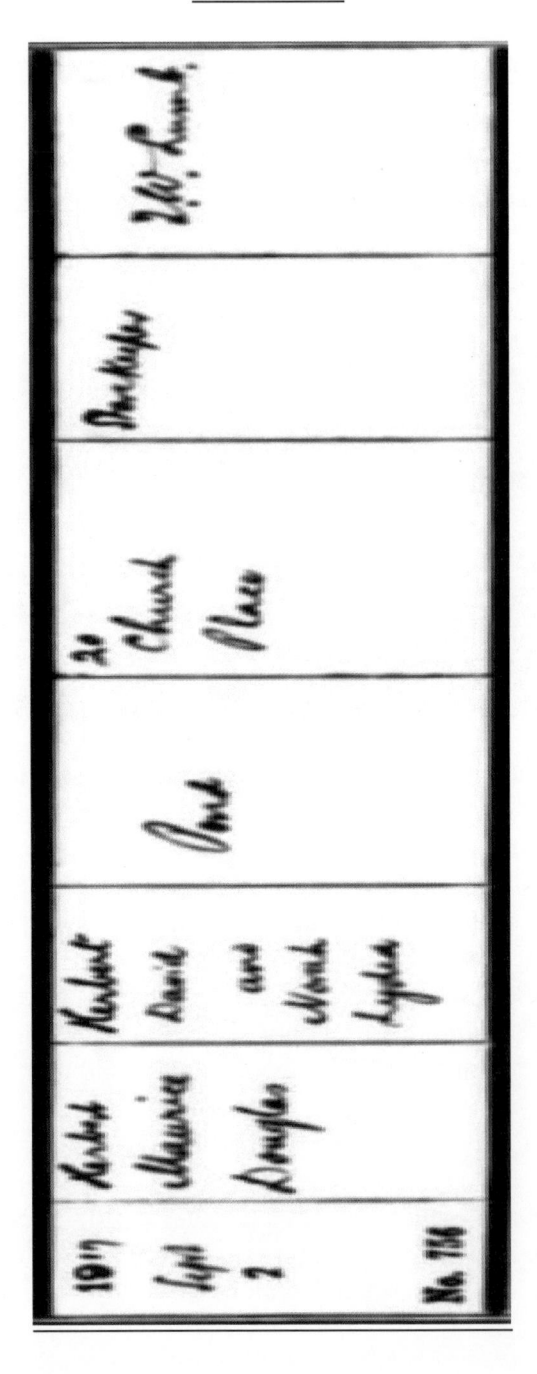

1917 Sept 2	Herbert Maurice Douglas	Herbert David and Sarah Hughes	Male	20 Church Place	Dockyard	W. Russel
No. 786						

In WW2 he was serving in the Royal Navy. The British Prisoner of War records shows that he was a Leading Supply Assistant with service number of MX57039 and a prisoner number of 168. He was in Camp Number O/9A in Spangenburg Bei Kassel, Germany.

<u>Prisoner of war record</u>

UK, British Prisoners of War, 1939-1945

View record

Name	H M D Pond
Rank	Leading Supply Assistant
Army Number	MX57039
Regiment	Naval Forces : Officers & Ratings
POW Number	168
Camp Type	Oflag
Camp Number	O/9A
Camp Location	Spangenburg Bei Kassel
Section	Naval Forces : Officers & Ratings

Later he married Edith Daisy Brewer on Saturday the 26th May 1945 in Trowbridge.
They then Emigrated on Thursday the 5th February 1953 to New Zealand to join the Royal New Zealand Navy.

They did have three children two sons and one daughter, but unable to trace them.

Herbert was Naturalized on Thursday the 23rd July 1981.

Record

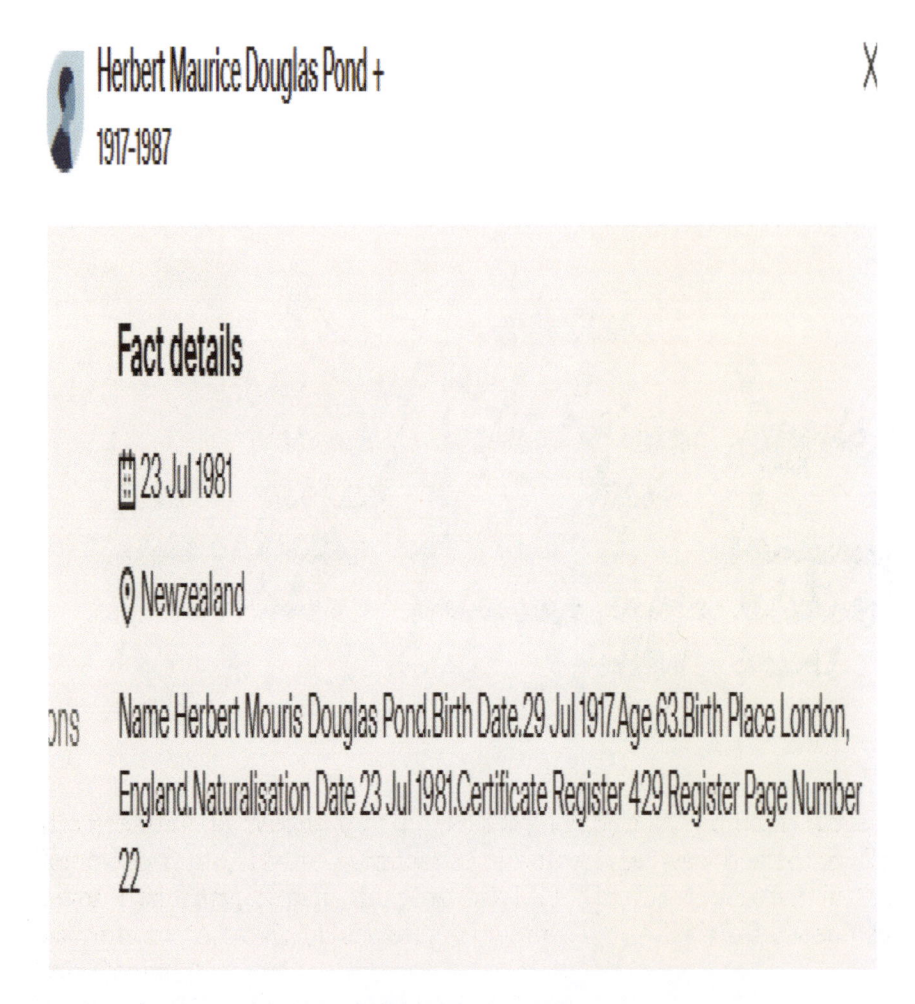

Herbert Maurice Douglas Pond +
1917-1987

Fact details

23 Jul 1981

Newzealand

Name Herbert Mouris Douglas Pond.Birth Date.29 Jul 1917.Age 63.Birth Place London, England.Naturalisation Date 23 Jul 1981.Certificate Register 429 Register Page Number 22

Herbert Maurice Douglas Pond died on Thursday the 8th October 1987 in New Zealand. His wife Edith died in 2002.

NORAH LYDIA FORD

Norah was born on Saturday the 1st November 1873 in Trowbridge to parents Eli and Jane Ford (nee Maslen).

On 1891 census she is aged 17 and living with her father who is listed as Widower and her twin brother Albert. (It is noted that he is on an 1881 census with the family, but she is not). The address was 11 Duke Street, Trowbridge.

In Q2 1896 in Melksham, Wiltshire she married Herbert David Pond. She died on Saturday the 29th May 1954 and was buried alongside her husband in Saint John's Churchyard in Trowbridge.

Probate

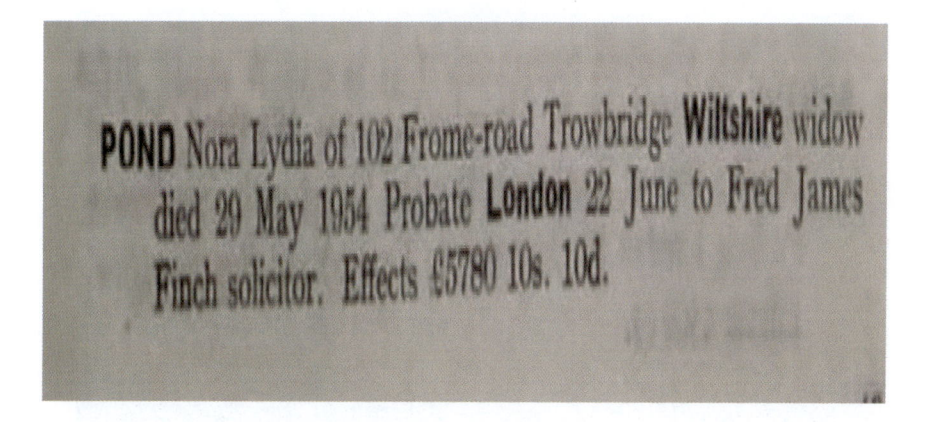

POND Nora Lydia of 102 Frome-road Trowbridge Wiltshire widow died 29 May 1954 Probate London 22 June to Fred James Finch solicitor. Effects £5780 10s. 10d.

Notes on her twin brother Albert

Records from his Attestation to join the Army on Saturday the 18th September 1915:-

His address before joining was 35 Mount Pleasant, Trowbridge.

He was aged 41 with the occupation of Labourer.

His Service number was 120340 in the 6th Labour Battalion, Royal Engineers.

He was married to Ada Louisa Doel (1879-1964) (who is next of kin) and had five children: Dorothy Minnie 1904-1980, Gladys May 1907-1981, Herbert Reginal 1910-1964, Sidney Albert 1911-1973 and Harry Stewart 1914-1936.

Below is a copy of a Telegraph dated Tuesday 2nd May 1916. It reads: "Stationary Hospital Rouen reports 120340 pioneer A. Ford 6th labour Battn. R.E. Dangerous ill ??? pneumonia, relatives may be visited, follow usual procedure, case at public expense".

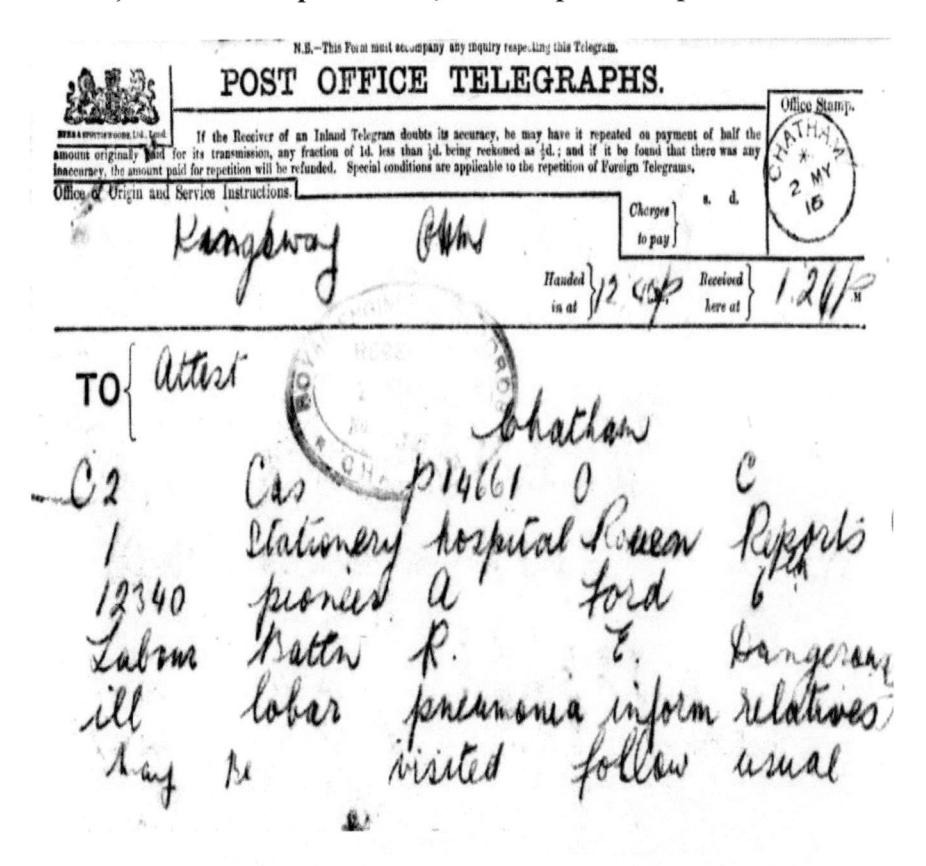

The next day on Wednesday the 3rd May 1916, Albert died in Rouen, Seine-Maritime, Haute-Normandie, France. He was buried in St. Sever Cemetery, Rouen, in plot A.20.20. On his headstone is the inscription: "A Loving Husband, A Father Kind, A Beautiful Memory Left Behind."
He is one of 3,083 servicemen buried there.
He was only in the Army for a total of 229 days.

Death record

FORD, Pnr. Albert, 120340. 6th Labour Bn. Royal Engineers. Died of pneumonia 3rd May, 1916. Age 42. Husband of Ada Louisa Ford, of 35, Mount Pleasant, Trowbridge, Wilts. A. 20. 20.

Commonwealth War Graves Record

In Memory Of
Pioneer

ALBERT FORD

Service Number: 120340

6th Labour Bn., Royal Engineers who died on 03 May 1916 Age 42

Husband of Ada Louisa Ford, of 35, Mount Pleasant, Trowbridge, Wilts.

A LOVING HUSBAND, A FATHER KIND A BEAUTIFUL MEMORY LEFT BEHIND

Remembered with Honour
ST. SEVER CEMETERY, ROUEN
A. 20. 20.

COMMONWEALTH
WAR GRAVES

COMMEMORATED IN PERPETUITY BY THE COMMONWEALTH
WAR GRAVES COMMISSION

GREAT GRANDPARENTS
WILLIAM HUDSON BRYARS & JESSIE FRANCIS ELIZABETH CLARKE

WILLIAM HUDSON BRYARS
William was born about 1850 in West Butterwick, Lincolnshire, to parents William and Mary Bryars (nee Hudson).
Aged 1 on the 1851 census he is with his parents, living in West Butterwick.
Next census in 1861 lists him as aged 11, with his parents and four siblings: Arthur 9, John Henry 7, twins Mary Adelaide and Gertrude aged 2, living in West Butterwick. He is listed as a "Farmers son."
Now aged 21 he is listed as "Assistant" on the 1871 census, in the household of Mr. John Wade at the address of Chemist Shop, 174 Warwick Street, Westminster, London. His occupation is "Assistant Dentist – Pharmacist."
In July 1889 in Barrow upon Soar, Leicestershire he married Jessie Frances Elizabeth Clarke.
Now aged 41 in 1891 he is with his wife and son William Hudson aged 6 months. They lived at 801 Attercliffe Road, in the Borough of Sheffield. His occupation was "Chemist."
On the 1901 census he is aged 51, with his wife and six children: William Hudson 10, Arthur Roy 8, **Ernest Harry 7 (your Grandfather)**, Mary Elizabeth 5, Frances Harriette 3 and John Fairfax 10 months. They were at 801 Attercliffe Road, in the Borough of Sheffield. His occupation was "Chemist – Drug."
Aged at 61 on the 1911 census he is with his wife and four children: Arthur, Mary, Frances and John. They were still at 801 Attercliffe Road, in the Borough of Sheffield. His occupation was "Chemist." His son Arthur is listed as "Student (Veterinary Surgeon)."
William died on Monday the 28th April 1913 in Sheffield and buried on Thursday the 1st May.

William Hudson Bryars in his Chemist shop

Notes and Pictures of their children

William Hudson, 30th September 1890 - 11th April 1959 in Madras, India.

William Hudson Bryars

Ernest Harry, 25ᵗʰ December 1893 – 1977.

Ernest Harry Bryars

Arthur Roy, 1894-1969. In 1923 he was living with his brother John Fairfax at 104 Lewin Road, Streatham, London.
Then in 1926 with his mother and brother John Fairfax at 104 Lewin Road, Streatham, London.
1931-32 he was living at 9 Buckleigh Road, Streatham, London.
I found the following notes on Arthur Roy Bryars on the Ancestry web site by another researcher:

Arthur Roy Bryars

Studio portrait of Roy and Harry Bryars

Arthur Roy Bryars, known as Roy, the second son of William and Jessie Bryars, never married but was apparently considered by his younger brother Fairfax to be the 'dare-devil' and 'black sheep' of his generation. He never qualified as a pharmaceutical chemist but worked as a dispenser at a chemist's shop in Streatham, and lived there for much of his life at 104 Lewin Road. He served in the King's Own Yorkshire Light Infantry in World War I: at the end of October 1917, a letter from Taylor and Newborn, one of the solicitors concerned with unravelling his mother's financial affairs, wrote to Lance Corporal A.R. Bryars 45195, D. Company, 14th K.O.Y.L.I., at Bury St. Edmunds. His brother Fairfax always maintained that he left the Army 'a full-blown private', but apart from this letter there is a photograph which shows him wearing his Lance Corporal's tape. He apparently served on the Western Front, and there is a slight possibility that he may have transferred to the Camel Corps for a time. Fairfax Bryars was wont to relate a story which he found highly amusing about his brother's wartime experiences. Roy Bryars, a large well-built man who later developed a double chin, was creeping round a haystack in Belgium, fully armed with rifle and packs, when he came face to face with an equally large German doing the same thing from the other side of the hayrick. They both took one look at each other and bolted in opposite directions.

Roy Bryars

Fairfax Bryars also recalled a day in the early 1920s when Roy suddenly suggested that the two of them should go to St. Malo for a holiday. They left immediately without booking, and apparently had a wonderful time which Fairfax Bryars referred to frequently for many years afterwards.

According to his sister Frances, Roy Bryars was bombed twice in Streatham during World War II, and was lucky to escape with his life, but a quantity of interesting family papers was destroyed.

Before his mother's death, Roy Bryars visited her and his sisters at Alton at Christmas, and although his presence 'livened things up', his jokes were not always well received by some members of the family. After Jessie Bryars' death, his visits ceased and he rarely wrote; he never married, and died at the end of the 1960s.

Harry and Roy Bryars, Enfield

Mary Elizabeth, 14th November 1895 – 1986.

Frances Anette, 1st March 1898 – 1986.

Frances Anette and Mary Elizabeth Bryars - 1979 in Alton

John Fairfax, 1st June 1900 – 30th January 1976.

John Fairfax and Frances Bryars

This picture is of Jessie Bryars on the right, Roy Fairfax on the left and Harry seated.

Back row L - R: Roy, John Fairfax and Jessie. Front row Harry

JESSIE FRANCES ELIZABETH CLARKE

Jessie was born on Thursday the 5th August 1858 in Barrow upon Soar, Leicestershire, to parents William and Elizabeth Clarke (nee Dakin).

She is aged 4 on the 1861 census, living with her parents and two siblings: Eleanor 4 and Mary Agnes Florence of 4 months. They lived in the village of Thurcaston, Leicestershire.

Then in the next census in 1871 she is aged 12, with her parents and three siblings: Eleanor 14, William Edmund 8 and Mary Jane of 8 months, living Roecliffe Farm, Newtown Linford, Leicestershire.

Jessie is aged 22 on the 1881 census, still with her parents and five siblings: William 18, Annie 13, Ernest 8 and Percy Reginald 6, living at Cossington Fields, Cossington, Leicestershire.

In July 1889 in Barrow upon Soar, Leicestershire she married William Hudson Bryars.

Jessie is listed in the 1911 White's Directory of Sheffield & Rotherham under Confectioners as being at 347 Sharrow Road, Sheffield.

347 Sharrow Road

In the London Electoral Register for 1924 she is living at 104 Lewin Road, Streatham. In the house was her son's Arthur Roy Clarke and John Fairfax Clarke.

On the 1939 register Jessie is listed as "Widow and Incapacitated", living with her daughter, Francis at 4 Park Close Road, Alton, Hampshire.

She died aged 87 on Tuesday the 1st October 1946 and her last address was 3 Welbourne Crescent, Sheffield. Her cremated remains are buried at Tinsley Park Cemetery, Sheffield, in plot Q10c which is the same as her husband.

Jessie Frances Elizabeth Clarke

Jessie Frances with her Granddaughter Norah Elizabeth Bryars

2X GREAT GRANDPARENTS
RICHARD PIDSLEY & SUSAN GARD / VEYSEY

RICHARD PIDSLEY
Richard was born about 1834 in Sowton, Devon, to parents Henry and Harriet Pidsley (nee Skinner).
In Q2 of 1859 Ottery Saint Mary, Devon he married Susan Gard (this was her second marriage as she was born Susan Veysey and then married Francis Gard who died in 1856).
They had a son **Richard (your Great Grandfather)** who was born on Wednesday the 5th December and baptised on Friday the 21st of 1860 in the district of Ottery Saint Mary.
On the 1861 census he is aged 26, living with his wife in Yonder Street, Ottery Saint Mary. His occupation was "Maltster employing one boy."
Richard aged 35 was buried on Thursday the 2nd July 1868 in Ottery Saint Mary.

SUSAN VEYSEY
Susan was baptised on Wednesday the 21st December 1825 in Honiton, Devon, to parents John and Julia Veysey (nee Newberry).
She was married in Q1 1847 in Honiton, Devon to Francis Gard.
Aged 25 in the 1851 census she is with her husband Francis, living in Awliscombe
Her husband Francis aged 35 was buried on the 16th January 1856 in Awliscombe, Devon.
Then in Q2 of 1859 Ottery Saint Mary, Devon she married Richard Pidsley.
Susan died on Sunday the 31st January and was buried on Thursday the 4th February 1869 nearly six months after her husband Richard died in Ottery Saint Mary.

Probate

PIDSLEY Susan. 23 April. The Will of Susan Pidsley late of Ottery St. Mary in the County of **Devon** Widow deceased who died 31 January 1869 at Ottery St. Mary aforesaid was proved at **Exeter** by the oaths

Effects under £100.

Their son Richard as stated on the census two years later, shows him as aged 10 and listed as "Nephew and **Orphan**" to the householder who was his uncle.

2X GREAT GRANDPARENTS
THOMAS TUCKER & MARY OTTON

THOMAS TUCKER
Thomas was born on Monday the 25th March and baptised on Sunday the 21st April 1833 in Stockland, Devon, to parents Robert and Mary Sarah Tucker (nee Fry).
He was aged 8 on the 1841 census living with his parents and five siblings: Timothy 20, James 15, Ann 14, Charles 10 and Mark 3. The house was in the village of Stockland.
In the 1851 census he is listed as "Boarder" in the household of his brother Timothy Tucker and his family. (Timothy was a "Blacksmith"). Thomas was a "Farm Labourer." The house was in the village of Stockland.
He was married in Q4 1858 in Exeter to Mary Otton.

Now aged 27 in 1861 he is with his wife and daughter **Mary Jane aged 2 (your Great Grandmother)**. They were living in Honiton, Devon and his occupation was "Wheelwright."

Now in 1871 he is aged 38, with his wife and four children: George 10, Charles 7, Harry 5 and Mark 2, living at 3 Nicholas Street, Bedminster, Bristol. His occupation now was "Carpenter."

His age on the 1881 census was given as 47 and is listed as "Boarder" in the house, which was in Tottenham, London. He was still listed as married, but there was no other member of his family with him. His occupation was "Carpenter."

Thomas died in Q4 1886 in Bedminster.

MARY OTTON

Mary was baptised on Sunday the 7th June 1835 in Honiton, Devon, to parents Henry and Jane Otton (nee Moore).

In the 1841 census she is aged 6, with her parents and two older siblings: Jane 14 and Henry 9. They lived in Ivy House Cottage in Honiton.

Mary is aged 17 on the next census in 1851 where she is listed as "House Servant". The householder was Thomas Knott, a "Chemist" with his family. Also, there was a cook and a nursemaid.

She was married in Q4 1858 in Exeter to Thomas Tucker.

Mary died in the same time period as her husband in Q4 1886 in Bedminster.

2X GREAT GRANDPARENTS
EPHRAIM POND & MARY ANN ORAM

EPHRAIM POND
Ephraim was born about 1826 in Trowbridge and was a twin, to parents Thomas and Ann Pond (Garrett).
Can find no record of his birth as his estimated age differed on each census, which was quite common in those days before people attended school.
In the 1841 census he is aged 15, living with his parents and six siblings: twins Charles and Catherine aged 20, his twin sister Leah 15, Enos 10, Ann 8 and Lydia 6. They lived in Trowbridge and from his father down to and including Leah, were all "Woollen Weavers."
In October 1858 he married Mary Ann Oram in Melksham, Wiltshire. They then had a son Frank A. on Thursday the 21st July 1864.
Ephraim is aged 47 on the 1871 census, with his wife and son Frank aged 6. They lived in Castle Street, Trowbridge where he was a "Brewer."
A second son **Herbert David (your Great Grandfather)** came along on Saturday the 30th May 1875.
In 1881 he was aged 60 and living with his wife and son Herbert aged 5. Their address was 50 Castle Street, Trowbridge with the occupation of a "Cloth Worker."
On the next census in 1891 he gave his age as 69, living with his wife and son Herbert aged 15, residing at 16 Polebarn Road, Trowbridge, He was listed as "Unemployed".
Now aged 78 he is with his wife living at 4 Castle Yard off Ashton Street, Trowbridge. He is not listed with a job, but his wife aged 62 is a "Mender Woollen Cloth Mill".
Ephraim was buried on Wednesday the 7th March 1906 in Trowbridge.

MARY ANN ORAM
Mary was baptised on Sunday the 18th November 1838 in Enfold, Wiltshire, to parents Thomas and Sarah Oram (nee Willis).

Baptism record

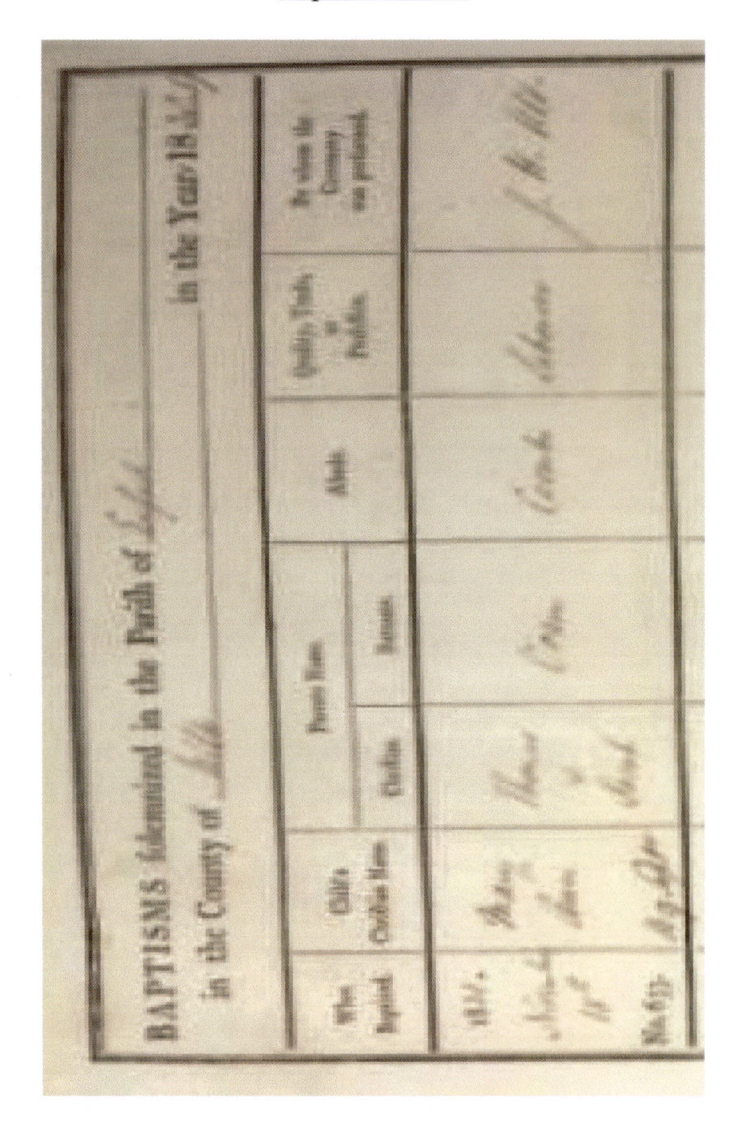

In October 1858 She married Ephraim Pond in Melksham, Wiltshire. Mary died about 1909 in Trowbridge.

2X GREAT GRANDPARENTS
ELI FORD & JANE MASLEN

ELI FORD
Eli was born in 1829 in Trowbridge, to parents John and Elizabeth Ford (nee Rolfe).

On the 1841 census he is aged 10 and living with his younger brother George aged 5, in his Grandparents house. His parents were in the house next door with Eli's six other siblings: Maria 15, Ephraim 15, Caroline 10, Clifford 5, Eliza 5 and Samuel 2. Living in Trowbridge.

On the next census in 1851 he gave his age as 22, living with his parents and four younger siblings: George 19, Clifford 17, Eliza 15 and Samuel 13. Living in Dursley Lane, Trowbridge, where he was a "Labourer."

Eli married Jane Maslen on Sunday the 17th October 1852 in Trowbridge.

Marriage record

He is aged 32 in 1861, with his wife and four children: John 7, James 5, Sarah Ann 4 and Frank 3, living in Stallard Street, Trowbridge, with the occupation of "Cloth Dresser" as was his wife.

Eli now aged 42 in 1871 was with his wife and seven children: John 17, Henry 15, Frank 13, Sarah 10, Fred 8, Mary 5 and Noah of 2 months, living in Balls Yard, Trowbridge, with the occupation of "Woollen Cloth worker".

They had a daughter Norah Lydia born on Wednesday the 9th September 1868 and baptised on Sunday the 18th October in Trowbridge, but this daughter died on Saturday the 14th May 1870.

Death record

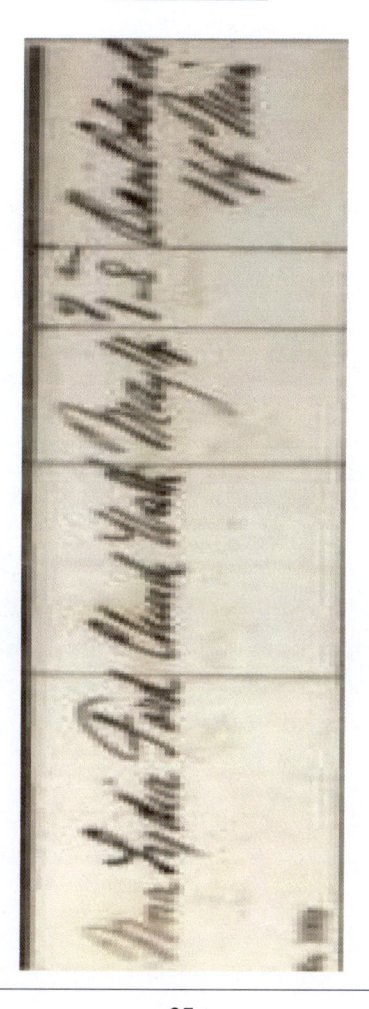

They then had a son Albert in 1873-1916.
Then another daughter who was named after the one that died, **Norah Lydia 1874-1954 (your Great Grandmother).**
On the 1881 census he is aged 52, a widower and with four of his children: Sarah 20 (a cloth washer), Mary 15 (a Cloth Piecer), Noah 10 (a Cloth Burler) and Albert 7, all living at 37 Duke Street, Trowbridge. Eli had no occupation against his name.
Then in 1891 he is aged 62 and with his two children Albert and Nora Lydia, living at 11 Duke Street, Trowbridge, where Eli and his son Albert are listed as "Cloth Workers".
Eli was buried on Thursday the 28th December 1899 in Trowbridge.

JANE MASLEN
Jane was born about 1833 in Trowbridge,
On the 1851 census she gave her age as 16 (but she was 18), living with her mother (Widow) in Trowbridge.
Jane married Eli Ford on Sunday the 17th October 1852 in Trowbridge.
It was noted then that Jane died in 1873, the same period and year as when their daughter Norah Lydia was born. So, was this due to childbirth?

2X GREAT GRANDPARENTS
WILLIAM BRYARS & MARY ANN HUDSON

WILLIAM BRYARS
William was baptised on Sunday the 15th September 1816 in Owston, Lincolnshire, to parents John and Elizabeth Bryars (nee Elwick).
On Wednesday the 14th June 1843 in Epworth, Lincolnshire, he married Mary Ann Hudson.
They had a daughter Mary Elizabeth in 1845 but she died in 1848.
Then they had a son John William in 1847 but he died in 1848.
Another son was born in 1850 who was **William Hudson (your Great Grandfather).**

On the 1851 census he is aged 34, with his wife and their son William aged 1, living in West Butterwick, Lincolnshire. Unable to read his occupation.

His age is 43 on the 1861 census, living with his wife and five children: William Hudson 11, Arthur 9, John Henry 7, twins Gertrude and Mary Adelaide 2, living in West Butterwick, Lincolnshire. His occupation is still hard to read but looks like "Castrator & Farmer of 21 Acres".

The County Directories for Lincolnshire in 1863, shows him as "Castrator".

County directory record

Trades and Professions.

Barnard John, miller
Batty James, grocer and draper
Bowman James Harrison, farmer
Brown Chatterton, farmer
Brown Jonathan, flax dealer
Brown Robert, farmer
Brown Robert Edward, farmer, West end
Brown William, jun., farmer
Bryars William, castrator
Burkinshaw Joseph, blacksmith
Butterick Jonathan, tailor

In the next census of 1871, his age is given as 54, with his wife and two children: Arthur 19 and Gertrude 12, living in North Street, West Butterwick, with occupation of "Farmer of 30 Acres".

Now aged 63 in 1881 he is with his wife and one daughter Mary aged 22, living in in North Street, West Butterwick, with occupation of "Castrator".

William died on Friday the 20th April 1888 and was buried in the graveyard of Saint Mary the Virgin, West Butterwick. Below are pictures of his grave. It is hard to read but it also lists his first two children, Mary Elizabeth and John William who died young as being buried with him.

<u>Their Gravestone</u>

MARY ANN HUDSON
Mary was born in 1823 in New Port, Yorkshire. Unable to locate her parents.
On the 1841 census she is aged 19, with her father and brother Henry 7, living in Belton, Lincolnshire.
On Wednesday the 14th June 1843 in Epworth, Lincolnshire, she married William Bryars.
Aged 68 on the 1891 census she is listed as "Widow living on own means" in West Butterwick.
She died just after the 1891 census and was buried in the same grave as her husband and two young children.

2X GREAT GRANDPARENTS
WILLIAM CLARKE & ELIZABETH DAKIN

WILLIAM CLARKE

William was born in 1824 in Mountsorrel, Leicestershire, to parents William and Elizabeth Clarks (nee Unknown).

On Friday, the **26th September** 1856 he had a daughter Eleanor, **then on Wednesday the 24th December married Elizabeth Dakin** in Cossington, Leicestershire.

The 1861 census shows him aged 36, with his wife and three children: Eleanor 4, **Jessie Frances Elizabeth 2 (your Great Grandmother)** and Mary of 4 months old. Also in the house was his mother-in law, Mary Dakin aged 76. William's occupation was "Farmer of 108 Acres employing two men". They lived in the village of Thurcaston, Leicestershire.

In 1871 his aged was given as 43, with his wife and four children: Eleanor 14, Jessie 12, William 8 and Mary of 8 months old. They lived at Roecliffe Farm, Newton Linford. His farm was now 200 Acres and he employed three men and two boys.

Now aged 50 in 1881 he was with his wife and six children: Jessie 22, William 18, Annie 13, Ernest 8, Percy 6 and Archibald 4. They lived at Cossington Fields, and he was a "Farmer with 270 Acres employing six men".

The census for 1891 gives his age as 66, with his wife and three children, living at The Grange, Cossington. He is still listed as "Farmer."

He is listed as "widower" on the 1901 census, living with his daughter Mary 30 and son Ernest 28, still living at The Grange, Cossington and "Farmer".

William died on Sunday the 29th July 1906 in Cossington.

His probate shows that he left £5215 15s 5d, which in 2022 the value is about **£675,766.**

Marriage record of William and Elizabeth

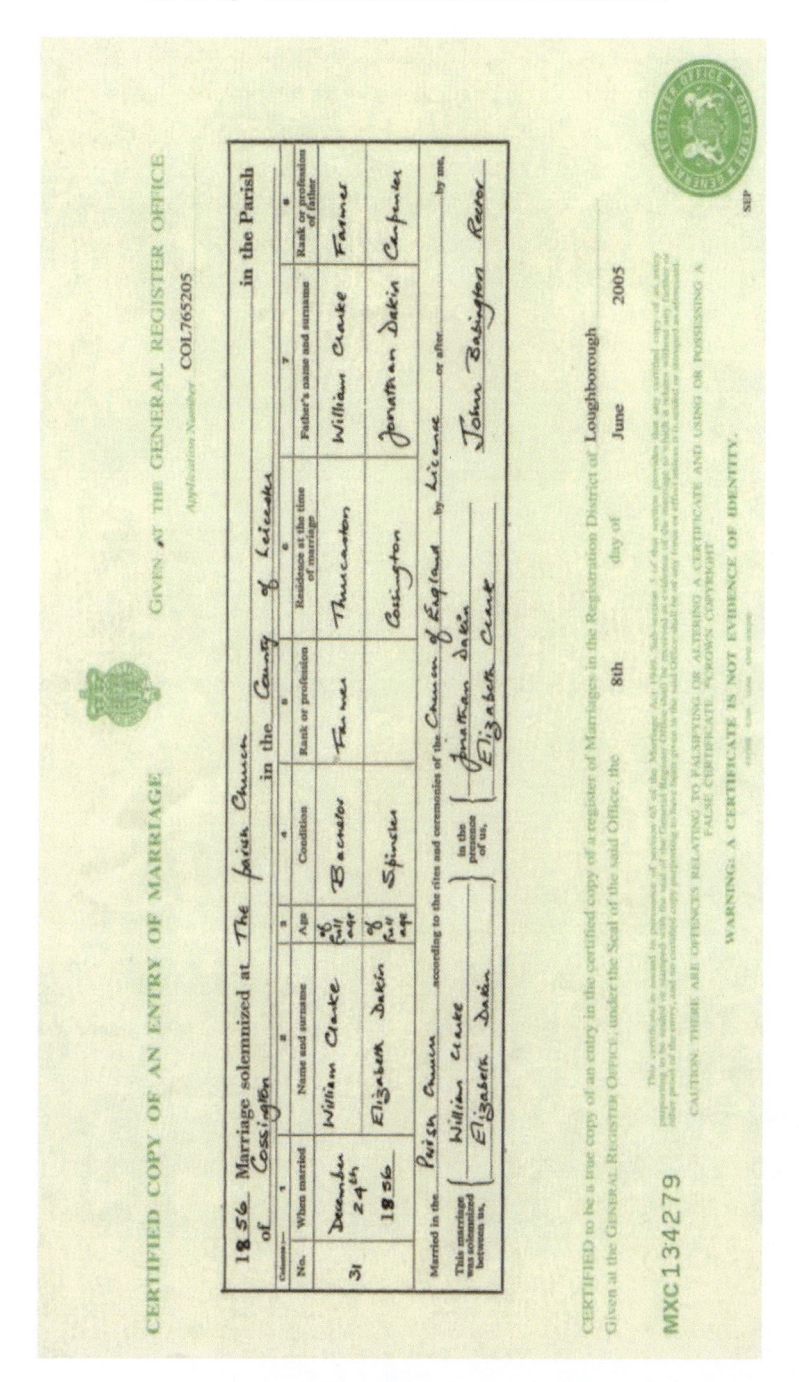

CERTIFIED COPY OF AN ENTRY OF MARRIAGE GIVEN AT THE GENERAL REGISTER OFFICE

Application Number COL765205

1856 Marriage solemnized at The Parish Church in the Parish of Cossington in the County of Leicester

No.	When married	Name and surname	Age	Condition	Rank or profession	Residence at the time of marriage	Father's name and surname	Rank or profession of father
31	December 24th 1856	William Craske	of full age	Bachelor	Farmer	Thrussington	William Craske	Farmer
		Elizabeth Dakin	of full age	Spinster		Cossington	Jonathan Dakin	Carpenter

Married in the Parish Church according to the rites and ceremonies of the Church of England by Licence or after, by us, John Babington Rector

This marriage was solemnized between us, { William Craske / Elizabeth Dakin } in the presence of us, { Jonathan Dakin / Elizabeth Craske }

CERTIFIED to be a true copy of an entry in the certified copy of a register of Marriages in the Registration District of Loughborough
Given at the GENERAL REGISTER OFFICE, under the Seal of the said Office, the 8th day of June 2005

MXC 134279

WARNING: A CERTIFICATE IS NOT EVIDENCE OF IDENTITY.
CAUTION: THERE ARE OFFENCES RELATING TO FALSIFYING OR ALTERING A CERTIFICATE AND USING OR POSSESSING A FALSE CERTIFICATE. ©CROWN COPYRIGHT

ELIZABETH DAKIN

Elizabeth was baptised on Saturday the 3rd September 1831 in Cossington, to parents Jonathan and Mary Dakin (nee Smith).

She is aged 10 on the 1841 census, with her parents and three older siblings: Mary 18, William, 16 and Edmund 12, living in Cossington.

Now aged 19, she is with her parents in Cossington.

Then on Wednesday the 24th December 1856 married William Clarke in Cossington, Leicestershire.

Elizabeth died in 1894 in Barrow upon Soar.

3X GREAT GRANDPARENTS
HENRY PIDSLEY & HARRIET SKINNER

HENRY PIDSLEY
Henry was baptised on Monday the 5th November 1804 in Topsham, Devon, to parents Richard and Susanna Pidsley (nee Fodden).
On Thursday, the 30th November 1826 he was married in Rockbeare, Devon to Harriet Skinner.
They had eleven children: Henry 1828, Susannah 1830, **Richard 1834 (your 2X Great Grandfather)**, Eliza 1836, Rose Ann 1838, Hellen 1840, William 1842, Thomas 1844, Edwin 1846, Amelia 1849 and James 1851.
In the 1851 census he is aged 46, living with his wife and all his eleven children. He was a "Farmer of 200 Acres employing five labourers". The address was "Court Farm" in Clist Saint George.
The 1861 census shows him as aged 56, with his wife and five children: Susannah, Rose Ann, Thomas, Edwin and Amelia. He now has "260 Acres and employing four labourers and one boy", still at "Court Farm" in Clist Saint George.
Henry died on Monday the 15th July 1861 in Clist Saint George.

<u>Probate</u>

PIDSLEY Henry.

Effects under £1,000.

3 August. The Will of Henry Pidsley formerly of Sowton but late of Clyst St. George both in the County of Devon Yeoman deceased who died on or about 15 July 1861 at Clyst St. George aforesaid was proved at **Exeter** by the oath of Harriet Pidsley of Clyst St. George aforesaid Widow the Relict and the sole Executrix.

HARRIET SKINNER
Harriet was baptised on Wednesday the 28th December 1803 in Aylesbeare, Devon to parents Robert and Susanna Skinner (nee unknown).
On Thursday, the 30th November 1826 she was married in Rockbeare, Devon to Henry Pidsley.
On the 1871 census is aged 67, a widow and living with her daughter Amelia in Topsham, Devon.
Harriet died in Q1 1877.

3X GREAT GRANDPARENTS
JOHN VEYSEY & JULIA NEWBERRY
Only record I could find for them was a marriage on Sunday the 29th March 1812 in Honiton, Devon.
They had a daughter **Susan in 1825 (your 2X Great Grandmother).**

3X GREAT GRANDPARENTS
ROBERT TUCKER & MARY FRY

ROBERT TUCKER
Robert was baptised on the 15th January 1792 in Dalwood, Devon, to parents William and Elizabeth Tucker (nee Spurway).
He had six siblings.
Then on Wednesday the 26th March 1817 in Colyton, Devon, he married Mary Fry.
They had twelve children: Timothy 1819-1887, Priscilla 1821-1884, George 1823-1884, James 1825-1902, Ann 1826-1908, Ann Hern 1827-1908, Robert 1828-1829, Charles 1830-1909, Charles James 1831-1909, Benjamin 1831-1880, **Thomas 1833 (your 2X Great Grandfather)**, Jane 1835-1835 and Mark 1838-1885.
In 1823 his occupation was "Blacksmith".
On the 1841 census he is aged 50, with his wife and six of his children, living in the district of Axminster, Dorset.
Then aged 59 in the next census of 1851 and with his wife in Stockland, Devon.
Robert died on Wednesday the 10th September 1856 in Stockland, Devon.

MARY FRY
Mary was baptised on the 16th October 1796 in Broadwinsor, Dorset. Then on Wednesday the 26th March 1817 in Colyton, Devon, she married Robert Tucker.

On the 1861 census she is aged 66, a widow, an invalid and listed as mother-in-law to the householder who was her daughter Ann, now married to Samuel Hern and their five children. Living in Stockland.

Now aged 75 in 1871 she is still a widow and listed as mother-in-law to the householder who was her daughter Elizabeth, now married to Joshua Tutton and their five children, living in Wells, Somerset.

In the 1881 census she is aged 84 a widow and listed as mother-in-law to the householder who was her daughter Mary, now married to Thomas Brooke, living in Spring Street, Bristol, Gloucestershire.

3X GREAT GRANDPARENTS
HENRY OTTON & JANE MOORE

HENRY OTTON
Henry was baptised on the 9th January 1785 in Awliscombe, Devon. He was married in November 1808 in Awliscombe, to Jane Moore. They had seven children: John 1829-1895, Ann 1822-1899, Harriet 1825-1900, Jane 1827-1897, Charles 1829-1911, Henry 1832-1899 and **Mary 1835-1915 (your 2x Great Grandmother).**

On the 1841 census he is aged 50, with his wife and three children: Jane 14, Henry 9 and Mary 6. He is listed as aged 66 on the 1851 census, with his wife and son Henry, living at Ivy House, Honiton, with the occupation of "Yeoman".

Then age 78 on the next census in 1861, he is with his wife and listed as a "Farmer of 14 acres", in Honiton.

Henry died in Q2 1862 in Honiton.

JANE MOORE
Jane was born about 1788 in Honiton.

She was married in November 1808 in Awliscombe, to Henry Otton. In the census for 1871 she is aged 81, a widow and living with her Grandson Charley Otton aged 21 and Granddaughter Mary Jane Tucker aged 12. They lived in Honiton and Jane is also listed as " Retired Dairy Woman."

3X GREAT GRANDPARENTS
THOMAS POND & ANN GARRETT

THOMAS POND
Thomas was baptised on the 7th February 1792 in North Bradley, Wiltshire, to parents Thomas and Martha Pond (nee Garrett).
On Monday the 28th September 1818 in North Bradley, he married Ann Garrett.
They had a son **Ephraim in 1826 (your 2 X Great Grandfather).**
Thomas died on the 4th September 1842 in Melksham, Wiltshire.

ANN GARRETT
Ann was baptised on the 27th August 1797 in North Bradley, Wiltshire, to parents Richard and Ann Garrett (nee Webb).
On Monday the 28th September 1818 in North Bradley, she married Thomas Pond.
Ann died on Monday the 26th February 1866 in North Bradley.

3X GREAT GRANDPARENTS
THOMAS ORAM & SARAH WILLIS

THOMAS ORAM
Thomas was baptised on Monday the 23rd November 1807, to parents Isaac and Anne Oram (nee Tailor).
On Saturday the 2nd November 1833 in Enford, Wiltshire, he married Sarah Willis.
They had a daughter on Sunday the 9th September 1838 named **Mary Ann (your 2X Great Grandmother).** Also, William 1835, Jane 1837, Emma 1841 and Sarah 1843.
He is aged 50 on the 1841 census, with his wife and daughter living in the parish of Edington, Wiltshire.
Thomas was buried on Saturday the 20th November 1847 in Pewsey, Wiltshire.

SARAH WILLIS
Sarah was baptised on Sunday the 6th June 1802, in Urchfont, Wiltshire. On the record it states, " Mothers name Elizabeth Willis and SINGLE."

On Saturday the 2nd November 1833 in Enford, Wiltshire, she married Thomas Oram.
Sarah died in Q3 1877 in Pewsey

3X GREAT GRANDPARENTS
JOHN FORD & ELIZABETH ROLFE

JOHN FORD
John was baptised on Friday the 27th November 1801 in Broughton Gifford, Wiltshire, to parents John and Mary Ford (nee Moore).
On Tuesday the 15th February 1820 in Trowbridge, he married Elizabeth Rolfe.

<u>Marriage record</u>

They had a son, **Eli in 1829 (your 2X Great Grandfather).**
 On the 1851 census he is aged 50, with his wife and five children: Eli 22, George 19, Clifford 17, Eliza 15 and Samuel 13. They lived in Dursley Lane, Trowbridge. He was a "Shearman" and his wife a "Weaver."
Then in 1861 he is aged 60, with his wife and two children: George 29 and Eliza 25, living in Trowbridge with an occupation of "Woollen Cloth Worker" as was his wife and daughter.
John was buried on Tuesday the 9th September 1873 in Trowbridge.

ELIZABETH ROLFE
Elizabeth was born on Sunday the 15th June 1800 in Trowbridge, to parents Samuel and Rosanna Rolfe (nee Frances).
On Tuesday the 15th February 1820 in Trowbridge, she married John Ford.
Elizabeth was buried on Tuesday the 6th April 1880 in Trowbridge.

3X GREAT GRANDPARENTS
JOHN BRYARS & ELIZABETH ELWICK

JOHN BRYARS
John was baptised on the 10th August 1789 in Belton in Axholme, Lincoln.
Then on Thursday the 21st December 1815 in Walkeringham, Nottingham he married Elizabeth Elwick.
They had a son **William in 1816 (your 2X Great Grandfather).**
On the 1851 census he is shown as aged 59 and with his wife, living at Clouds Lane, Belton, Lincolnshire, with occupation of "Castrator".
Then in 1861 he is aged 67 and with his wife, living at Clouds Lane, Belton, Lincolnshire, with occupation of "Farmer".
John died on Thursday the 13th May 1869 in Clouds Lane, Belton, Lincoln.

ELIZABETH ELWICK
Elizabeth was baptised on the 12th May 1793 in Walkeringham, Nottingham, to parents William and Sarah Elwick (nee Spencer).
Then on Thursday the 21st December 1815 in Walkeringham, Nottingham she married John Bryars.
She died on Saturday the 15th May in 1869 in West Butterwick, Lincolnshire.

3X GREAT GRANDPARENTS
JONATHAN DAKIN & MARY SMITH

JONATHAN DAKIN

Jonathan was baptised on the 28th January 1798 in Sileby, Leicestershire, to parents Thomas and Elizabeth Dakin (nee Marshall).

On Tuesday the 19th December 1820 in Seagrave, Leicestershire, he married Mary Smith.

They had five children: Mary 1822, William 1824, Jonathan 1827, Edmund 1829 and **Elizabeth 1831 (your 2X Great Grandmother).**

He is aged 45 on the 1841 census, with his wife and four of the children: Mary, William, Edmund and Elizabeth, living in Barrow upon Soar. His occupation was "Carpenter."

Then at the age of 1851 he was with his wife and daughter Elizabeth, living in Cossington as a "Carpenter".

Jonathan died on Friday the 21st December 1860.

Probate

DAKIN Jonathan.   21 February.   The Will of Jonathan Dakin late of Cossington in the County of **Leicester** Carpenter deceased who died 21 December 1860 at Cossington aforesaid was proved at **Leicester** by the oaths of William Dakin of Cossington aforesaid Carpenter the Son and William Cuffling of Swithland in the said County Farmer two of the Executors.

Effects under £600.

MARY SMITH

Mary was born about 1786 in Seagrave, Leicestershire. Unable to find parents.

On Tuesday the 19th December 1820 in Seagrave, Leicestershire, she married Jonathan Dakin.

In the 1861 she is listed as 76, Widow and the mother-in-law of the householder who was her daughter Elizabeth and her family, living in Thurcaston.

Mary died in 1870 in Barrow upon Soar.

4X GREAT GRANDPARENTS
RICHARD PIDSLEY & SUSANNA FODDEN

RICHARD PIDSLEY
Richard was born about 1755.
On the 31st October 1792 in Topsham, Devon he married Susanna Fodder.
They had two children: Peter 1801-1843 and **Henry 1805-1861 (your 3X Great Grandfather).**
Richard died in Q4 1842 and buried in Saint Michael and All Angels Churchyard in Sowton, Devon.
His son Peter and wife Susanna are buried in the same grave.

Gravestone

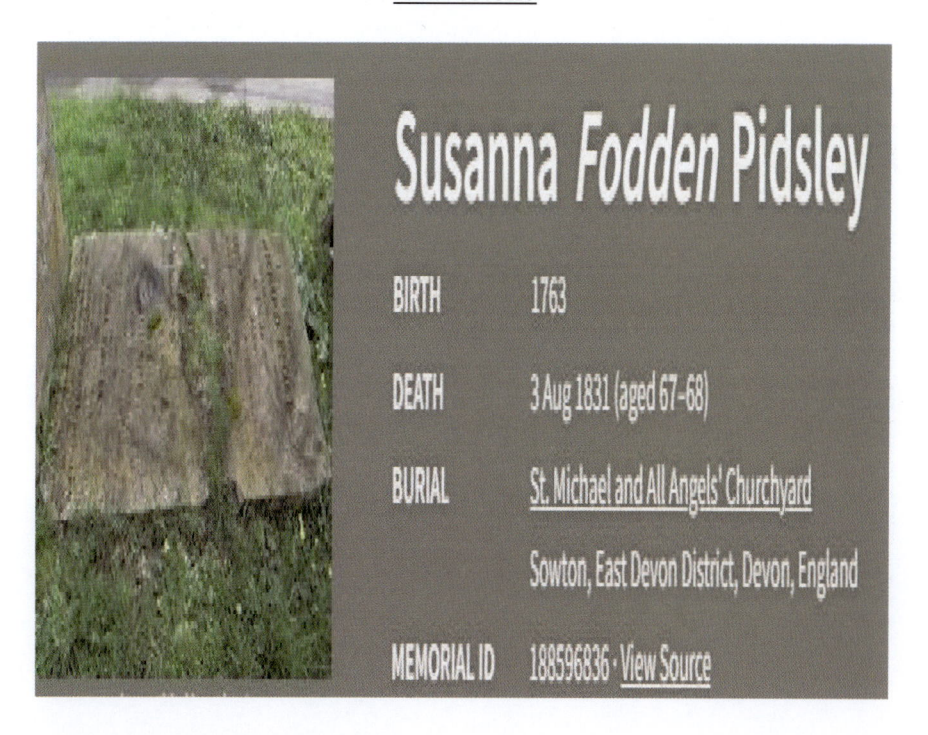

Susanna Fodden Pidsley

BIRTH: 1763

DEATH: 3 Aug 1831 (aged 67-68)

BURIAL: St. Michael and All Angels' Churchyard, Sowton, East Devon District, Devon, England

MEMORIAL ID: 188596836 · View Source

SUSANNA FODDEN
Susanna was born about 1763.
On the 31st October 1792 in Topsham, Devon she married Richard Pidsley.

She died on Wednesday the 3rd August 1831 and buried in Saint Michael and All Angels Churchyard in Sowton, Devon.

4X GREAT GRANDPARENTS
WILLIAM TUCKER & ELIZABETH SPURWAY

WILLIAM TUCKER
William was baptised on the 18th May 1758 in Dalwood, Devon, to parents Richard and Mary Tucker (nee Willis).
On the 27th February 1783 in Dalwood, he married Elizabeth Spurway.
They had several children one being **Robert in 1792 (your 3X Great Grandfather)**.
William died on Sunday the 7th April 1805 in Dalwood.

ELIZABETH SPURWAY
Elizabeth was baptised on the 3rd March 1765 in Dalwood, to parents Richard and Elizabeth Spurway (nee unknown)
On the 27th February 1783 in Dalwood, she married William Tucker.

4X GREAT GRANDPARENTS
THOMAS POND & MARTHA GARRETT

THOMAS POND
Thomas was born about 1765 in North Bradley, Wiltshire, to parents John and Mary Pond (nee Breacher).
On the 28th August 1785 in North Bradley, he married Martha Garrett.

Marriage record

No. 173.

Thomas Pond — of this Parish Batchelor — and Martha Garrett of this Parish Spinster — were Married in this Church by Banns — this twenty eighth Day of August — in the Year One Thousand Seven Hundred and Eighty five — By me Edw Duncan — Curate.

This Marriage was solemnised between Us { The Mark ✕ of Thomas Pond. The Mark + of Martha Garrett.

In the Presence of { John Butcher Jas Francis

They had eight children: John 1786, Mary 1787, William 1788, Betty 1790, Thomas 1792 **(your 3X Great Grandfather)**, Rebecca 1794, Sarah 1806 and Catherine 1807.
Thomas died about 1838 in North Bradley.

MARTHA GARRETT
Martha was baptised on the 21st March 1763 in North Bradley, to parents **Christopher and Sarah Garrett (nee Bridges).**
On the 28th August 1785 in North Bradley, she married Thomas Pond. Unable to find a death record for her.

4X GREAT GRANDPARENTS
RICHARD GARRETT & ANN WEBB

RICHARD GARRETT
Richard was baptised on the 13th April 1760 in North Bradley, to parents **Christopher and Sarah Garrett (nee Bridges).**
In 1762 Richard was joined with a sibling Martha Garrett.

NOTES

It is noticed at this stage that there is a similar occurrence to one earlier in this family tree. In that this Martha who is sister to Richard is the same Martha in the previous record who was married to Thomas Pond. Therefore, Richard Garrett and Martha Garrett have the same parents which was like your Grandparents Beatrice Lydia Rose Pond and Lily Florence Pond.

On the 12th July 1781 in Steeple Ashton, Wiltshire, he married Ann Webb.
In 1797 they had a daughter Ann **(your 3X Great Grandmother)**
Richard died in Q1 1800 in North Bradley.

ANN WEBB
Ann was born about 1762 in North Bradley.
On the 12th July 1781 in Steeple Ashton, Wiltshire, she married Richard Garrett.
Ann died on Sunday the 30th September 1810 in North Bradley.

4X GREAT GRANDPARENTS
ISAAC ORAM & ANNE TAILOR

ISAAC ORAM
Isaac was baptised on the 14th March 1741 in Edington, Wiltshire.
On the 27th December 1770 in Edington, he married Anne Tailor.
They had a son Thomas in 1790 **(your 3X Great Grandfather)**.
Isaac died on Wednesday the 9th May 1821 in Edington.

ANNE TAILOR
Anne was baptised on the 15th January 1745 in North Wraxall, Wiltshire.
On the 27th December 1770 in Edington, she married Isaac Oram.
Anne buried nearly six months later than her husband on Wednesday the 7th November 1821 in Edington.

4X GREAT GRANDPARENTS
UNKNOWN & ELIZABETH WILLIS

UNABLE TO FIND ANY RECORDS FOR HER.

4X GREAT GRANDPARENTS
JOHN FORD & MARY MOORE

JOHN FORD
John was born about 1773 in Wiltshire.
On the 12th November 1792 in Upton Scudamore, Wiltshire he married Mary Moore.
They had three children: Hannah 1792-1868, Rebecca 1797-1852 and in 1801 they had a son **John (your 3X Great Grandfather)**.

MARY MOORE
Mary was baptised on the 25th January 1767 in Upton Scudamore, Wiltshire, to parents John and Mary Moore (nee Blanchett).
On the 12th November 1792 in Upton Scudamore, Wiltshire she married John Ford.

4X GREAT GRANDPARENTS
SAMUEL ROLFE & ROSANNA FRANCES

SAMUEL ROLFE
Samuel was baptised on the 30th September 1781 in Berwick-Saint James, Wiltshire.
On Monday the 17th March 1800 in Trowbridge, he married Rosanna Frances.
They had a daughter **Elizabeth on Sunday the 15th June 1800 (your 3X Great Grandmother)**.
He is listed on the 1841 census as aged 60, with his wife and **Eli Ford aged 10 (your 2X Great Grandfather)** and his sibling George Ford aged 5. Eli's parents and other siblings were living in the house next door. They were living in Trowbridge.
Samuel died in 1842 in the district of Pewsey, Wiltshire.

ROSANNA FRANCES
Rosanna was born about 1776 in Wiltshire.
On Monday the 17th March 1800 in Trowbridge, she married Samuel Rolfe.
Rosanna was buried on Thursday the 8th February 1844 in Trowbridge.

4X GREAT GRANDPARENTS
WILLIAM ELWICK & SARAH SPENCER

WILLIAM ELWICK
William was born about 1753 in Walkeringham, Nottinghamshire.
On the 29th January 1789 in Walkeringham he married Sarah Spencer, to parents William and Mary Elwick (nee Garland)
They had eight children: Robert 1789, Mary 1791, Elizabeth 1793 **(your 3X Great Grandmother)**, Sarah 1795, Nancy 1797, Susannah 1799, Charlotte 1801 and William 1804.
William died in 1817 in Walkeringham.

SARAH SPENCER
Sarah was baptised on the 27th November 1763 in Walkeringham, to parents Samuel and Elizabeth Spencer (Keyworth).
On the 29th January 1789 in Walkeringham she married William Elwick.
Sarah died in Q2 1840 in Gainsborough, Lincolnshire.

4X GREAT GRANDPARENTS
THOMAS DAKIN & ELIZABETH MARSHALL

THOMAS DAKIN
Thomas was born about 1768 in Sileby, Leicestershire. Unable to trace parents.
On the 13th February 1793 in Sileby he married Elizabeth Marshall.
They had a son **Jonathan in 1796 (your 3X Great Grandfather)**.

ELIZABETH MARSHALL
Elizabeth was baptised on the 9th May 1773 in Sileby, to parents Thomas and Jane Marshall (nee Taylor).
On the 13th February 1793 in Sileby she married Thomas Dakin.

~~~

5X GREAT GRANDPARENTS
RICHARD TUCKER & MARY WILLIS

RICHARD TUCKER
Richard was baptised on the 6th July 1724 in Trowbridge, Wiltshire.
On the 17th June 1745 he married Mary Willis in Stockland, Devon.
They had nine children: Fanny 1745, John 1748, Dorothy 1753, Joanna 1754, Thomas 1754, **William 1758 (your 4X Great Grandfather)**, Sarah 1761, Joan 1765 and James 1769.
He died about 1805.

MARY WILLIS
Mary was baptised on the 1st August 1722 in Bridport, Dorset.
On the 17th June 1745 she married Richard Tucker in Stockland, Devon.
She died in 1779 in Dalwood.

5X GREAT GRANDPARENTS
RICHARD SPURWAY & ELIZABETH surname unknown

RICHARD SPURWAY
Richard was born on the 21st July
ELIZABETH surname unknown

5X GREAT GRANDPARENTS
JOHN POND & MARY BREACHER

JOHN POND
John was baptised on the 24th February 1735 in Shaftsbury, Dorset.
On the 15th February 1763 he married Mary Breacher.
They had a son **Thomas in 1765 (your 4X Great Grandfather).**
John was buried on Wednesday the 14th October 1829 in Motcombe, Dorset.

Death record

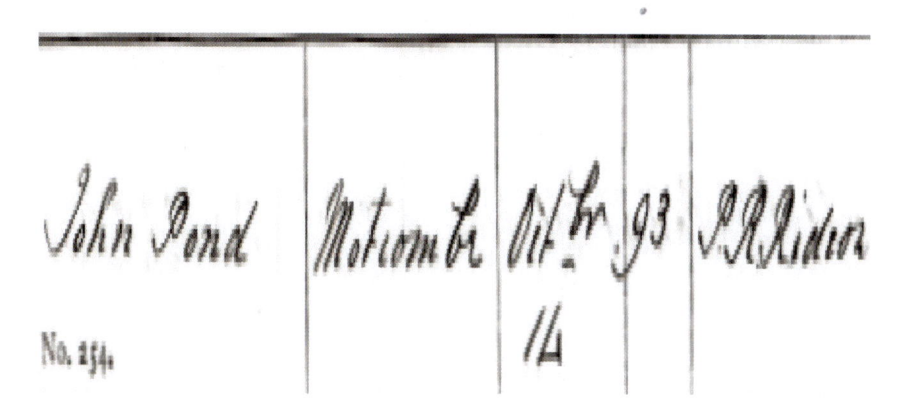

[handwritten record: John Pond | Motcomb | Oct 93 | ... | No. 254 | 14]

MARY BREACHER
Mary was baptised on the 28th December 1738 in Semley, Dorset.
On the 15th February 1763 she married John Pond.
Mary was buried on Sunday the 4th September 1814 in Semley.

5X GREAT GRANDPARENTS
CHRISTOPHER GARRETT & SARAH BRIDGES

CHRISTOPHER GARRETT
Christopher was born about 1728 in North Bradley.
On the 30th September 1753 in North Bradley, he married Sarah Bridges.
They had a son **Richard in 1760 (your 4X Great Grandfather and married to Ann Webb)** and then a daughter Martha **1762 (your 4X Great Grandmother married to Thomas Pond)**.
They also had James 1754, Elizabeth 1766, John 1769, Mary 1772 and Robert 1776.
Christopher was buried on the 21st February 1797 in North Bradley.

SARAH BRIDGES
Sarah was baptised on the 26th October 1736 in North Bradley.
On the 30th September 1753 in North Bradley, she married Christopher Garrett.
Sarah was buried on the 23rd April 1797 in North Bradley.

5X GREAT GRANDPARENTS
JOHN MOORE & MARY BLANCHETT

JOHN MOORE
John was baptised on the 4th January 1729 in Bromham, Wiltshire, to parents John and Deborah Moor/Moore (nee Amor)
On the 5th October 1760 in Lacock, Wiltshire he married Mary Blanchett.

Marriage record

They had a daughter **Mary (your 4X Great Grandmother).**

MARY BLANCHETT
On the 5th October 1760 in Lacock, Wiltshire she married John Moore.
Mary died in 1811 in Bradford, Wiltshire.

5X GREAT GRANDPARENTS
WILLIAM ELWICK & MARY GARLAND

WILLIAM ELWICK
William was baptised on the 30th December 1719 in Misterton, Nottinghamshire, to parents William and Sarah Elwick (nee Standring).
He later had a brother Edward born late in 1720 but died on the 16th December of the same year.
Then another brother, Robert was born on the 11th April 1726 in Walkeringham.
But just over two months later his father died.
William then married Mary Garland on the 17th September 1750 in Fledborough, Nottingham.
They had two children: Sarah 1751-1830 and William 1752-1817 **(your 4X Great Grandfather).**
He died in 1764.

MARY GARLAND
Mary was born in 1729 in Morton, Gainsborough, Lincolnshire.
Mary then married William Elwick on the 17th September 1750 in Fledborough, Nottingham.
Mary died on the 28th November 1753 in Misterton, Nottinghamshire.

5X GREAT GRANDPARENTS
SAMUEL SPENCER & ELIZABETH KEYWORTH

SAMUEL SPENCER
Samuel was baptised on the 31st January 1733 in Walkerington, Nottinghamshire

On the 2nd December 1760 in Walkerington he married Elizabeth Keyworth.

They had ten children: John 1761, **Sarah 1763-1840 (your 4X Great Grandmother)**, Samuel 1766-1771, George 1768-1771, George 1772-1863, William 1775-1846, Richard 1777-1846, Charles 1778-1863, Thomas 1780 and James 1781.

Samuel died on Sunday the 7th February 1819 in Walkeringham.

Gravestone

ELIZABETH KEYWORTH
Elizabeth was born on the 15th January 1738 in Walkeringham, to parents William and Ann Keyworth (nee Mails).
On the 2nd December 1760 in Walkerington she married Samuel Spencer.
Elizabeth died on Thursday the 5th November 1812 in Walkeringham and is buried in the same grave as her husband.

5X GREAT GRANDPARENTS
THOMAS MARSHALL & JANE TAYLOR

THOMAS MARSHALL
Thomas was born about 1740
On the 14th April 1760 in Sileby, he married Jane Taylor.
They had a daughter **Elizabeth in 1773 (your 4X Great Grandmother).**

JANE TAYLOR
Jane was born about 1740 in Leicestershire.
On the 14th April 1760 in Sileby, she married Thomas Marshall.

6X GREAT GRANDPARENTS
JOHN MOOR/MOORE & DEBORAH AMOR

JOHN MOOR/MOORE
John was baptised on the 1st May 1695 in Lacock, Wiltshire.
On the 16th January 1726 in Devizes, Wiltshire he married Deborah Amor.
In 1729 they had a son **John (your 5X Great Grandfather)**.

DEBORAH AMOR
Deborah was baptised on the 21st February 1700 in Bromham, Wiltshire.
On the 16th January 1726 in Devizes, Wiltshire she married John Moor/Moore.

6X GREAT GRANDPARENTS
WILLIAM ELWICK & SARAH STANDRING

WILLIAM ELWICK
William was baptised on the 16th December 1688 in Misterton, Nottinghamshire, to parents John and Elizabeth Elwick (nee Grays).
His mother died when he was only four.
On the 31st January 1711 in Misterton, he married Sarah Standring.
They had eight children: John 1713-1784, twins Sarah and George in 1714 but both died in the same year, Thomas 1716-1764, Anne 1718 but died in same year, William 1719-1764 **(your 5X Great Grandfather)**, Edward 1720 but died same year, and Robert 1726-1753.
William died on the 31st July 1726 in Misterton.

SARAH STANDRING
Sarah was born on the 9th June 1683 in Misterton.
On the 31st January 1711 in Misterton, she married William Elwick.
Sarah died on the 18th March 1744 in Misterton.

6X GREAT GRANDPARENTS
WILLIAM KEYWORTH & ANN MAILS

WILLIAM KEYWORTH
William was born 5th April 1702 in South Leverton, Nottinghamshire.
At some stage he married Ann Mails.
They had a daughter Elizabeth in 1738 **(your 5X Great Grandmother).**
William died in Q4 1790 in Ollerton, Nottinghamshire.

ANN MAILS
Ann was born about 1699 in Swinderby, Lincolnshire.
She died in Q1 1763 in Rufford, Nottinghamshire.

7X GREAT GRANDPARENTS
JOHN ELWICK & ELIZABETH GRAYS

JOHN ELWICK
John was born in 1661 in Misterton, Nottinghamshire.
He must have married Elizabeth before 1687 as from then they had two son's, John born on the 22nd August 1687 but died a week later on the 29th and William born on the 16th December 1688-1726 (your 6X Great Grandfather).
John died on the 31st July 1726 in Misterton.

ELIZABETH GRAYS
Elizabeth was born 1670 in Misterton.
She was buried in June 1692 in Ottringham, Yorkshire.

Printed in Great Britain
by Amazon